Cathy & Jim's
Dover to Outer Hebrides Cycle

March 20th to April 2nd
and
April 19th to May 18th 2017

Cathy & Jim's
Dover to Outer Hebrides Cycle

By
Jim Beard

Edited and honed

By Cathy Beard

Dedication

To our Fathers

We travelled with their spirits. They never knew each other but we know they would have loved to have seen our country in this simple way

From Near France to Near Iceland: Our Adventure

Our passage was mainly by Sustrans National Cycle Routes both fair and rough, from Dover in the South East to The Outer Hebrides in the extreme North West.

This is not an instruction manual but it should give you a feel of the thrills, spills, ills and pills that arise when old people take to the road.

The 800-mile trail took us through the eastern counties, under The Thames, over The Humber Bridge, round The North York Moors, along Hadrian's Wall, over The Pennines, over The Southern Uplands of Scotland and island hopping to The Outer Hebrides

INTRODUCTION

We had been waiting for our dog to die so we could take on this adventure. I know it sounds harsh. Our beloved Moidie was pretty rough (or was that gruff?) back in 2012. In anticipation of her demise back then, we bought sturdy Cube touring bikes for cycling fun but they were not compatible with an ailing dog. With Moidie kennelled at friends, we tried them out on a weeklong cycle from home to Amsterdam in 2012. Thereafter, for the last 5 years, they have been shed-stuff that ensured we performed yoga contortions to reach various gardening implements.

We are a very happily married couple that consider ourselves as walkers rather than cyclists. Cathy was 63 and I, Jim was 64, thinking, *"will she still need me? Will she still feed me?"* We had travelled much of the world together but hold our own land in the highest regard. The more we see of it, the more we know there is to see!

Our love of adventures hark back to our individual childhoods where Cathy cantered to primary school on imaginary horses and the police were intending to drag a pond for the four-year-old-me just before I returned home. Sports had kept us fit through our working life and our retirement 10 years ago saw us on trails beginning with The Essex Way, progressing through Wainwright's Coast to Coast and going onto making our own way from Land's End to John O'Groats in 2011. We consider the Coast to Coast the finest, most-varied walk in the world and hold our Land's End to John O'Groats walk as our best-ever adventure.

Friends had suggested it took 6 years to forget the hard toil of the long walk in order to be mad enough to attempt another big adventure, but most knew it was just a matter of time before we were off again. For us, it was a matter of giving Moidie-pup the best end-of-life years we owed her, then setting our sights on the dog-less freedom.

It began with the intention of Cathy running the whole length of the land with me as support on a bicycle. Cathy took up running in her thirties, fairing well as a Colchester Harrier for many years, and reaching Eastern Counties level in her time. I, on the other hand, am a worn out sportsman after an amateur career that becomes greater with every year since I retired. Arthritic hips and ankle allow me not to prove my ineptitude. Cathy's running of this mileage was planned to hone her to peak fitness as she would move up to a new age-group (over 65) in 20 months time.

In terms of planning, we chose to stick to Sustrans routes. Sustrans is a UK sustainable transport charity. Its flagship project is the National Cycle Network, which has created over 14,000 miles of signed cycle routes throughout the UK, but about 70% of the network is on previously existing, mostly minor roads, on which motor traffic will be encountered. You may have seen the blue, numbered signs, bolted to an existing signpost, with a picture of a bike on it.

We began with a great bunch of maps, which, once used, were posted back home (actually to our local friend, Sarah, rather than the Royal Mail Keepsafe arrangement we use when away). The journey through Kent was nearly pre-planned to follow CR (Cycle Route) 16 to its connection with the mighty CR1 although changes were made on the hoof. The remainder was loosely planned in a manner that assured us of the possibility of success without any specific path. Planning was done each night for the following day. As an ex-geography teacher with hundreds of field trips under her trim belt, Cathy controlled the maps. I had beer to drink.

The laminated sign on Cathy's back read "DOVER to CAPE WRATH" but we had no real idea where it would end. London? Cambridge? Carlisle? So, when we left our house by cycling to the station, we had no clear idea as to how this would turn out. Determination was there, definitely, but certainty? This was an adventure, so the only certainty was the uncertainty.

One of the stranger Sustrans Route Signs (River Nith, Scotland)

Right, here is where I get my excuses in early. You have already heard that we are old; but, also, we are not cyclists; our bikes were heavy tourers (17kg unloaded) and we would be carrying all our own camping gear. So, we were never going to be fast and the daily mileage would be minimal. So it was. The decision against a lightweight road bike (a Scultra is just over 4kg) was the terrain we would cross. Old railway lines and tow-paths would shake a light bike to bits, so we were recommended The Cube Tourer SL by the cutely named Life Cycle of Bildeston. (Or just gullible enough to fall for it? Only time would tell.)

My failing eyesight is not an excuse but a matter of fact you should be aware of. I have retinitis pigmentosa that kills off cells within my eyes. There is no known cure although that does not stop a range of experts calling me for examinations they hail as "very interesting'. It is hereditary (like diarrhoea, it runs in your genes?!?) and degenerative. In some ways, it leads me to do things just because it might be my last chance, but I never think like that. I do know I should be more cautious, but I am not like that either. I use this ailment as a point of humour rather than a blight. Cathy understands it and is now programmed to yell "stone" of "pothole" or 'tree-root" at the appropriate moments. Now let us get back to the plot.

Everyone we had talked to "had a friend" who had cycled from Land's End to John O'Groats in 10 days. We hail such feats, congratulate those fine folk and have been fortunate enough to keep their company for a while when walking that way, but we were never in their league. Nor did we have light racers; keep to fast routes; have pre-booked accommodation or have support vehicles to transport our gear. In our youth and quite separately, we had both cycled 100 miles in a day. It nearly killed us and took ages to recover from the agony. We were going to do this thing (whatever shape it would take) at our pace. That did not mean it was not arduous.

I kept a diary, the contents of which have been poured into this book with very little dilution. So, be warned, it carries all the puns that amused me on the way. Actually only the written ones; Cathy had to suffer far more verbal garbage as we went. It will also include inconsistency of tense, which is something Mr Payne, my English teacher tolerated rather than corrected, for which I thank him. The factual inaccuracies are only deliberate through ignorance, an attribute gained through age and the need to make things up to enable the dull me to appear more interesting.

This will not be a manual for anyone to follow. We never found one for this specific trip ourselves. It contains no maps, no specific directions and no outright instructions. What I can promise is the truth. I wrote as I felt, how we struggled, what delighted us and how truly wonderful our nation remains. One other factor that should become abundantly clear is my love for my Cathy.

It has been recommended that, by reading just a few days at a time, it will help you take the journey with us. It is not a one-sit-read book, so come and take to the road with us.

Ready?

The Diary

Fri Mar 24 2017 From Dover (after arriving from Home by train)

Joe was rather strange. He liked being strange but he was, is and ever will be normal. Apart, that is, for one, eery fact: he carries with him a framed picture of his house. It is a two-up-two-down abode, painted pink in a row of others that are not (pink). Why the framed picture? We never dared to ask.

  Joe made conversation and weak jokes (I should know) on the Stratford International Express to Dover Priory. He proudly walked us to his house as it was on our way, telling us that he gave up teaching for a place in industry because the pupils had pilloried him. We feared that the scars still showed.

On our own at last. Not really, Kent does not actually allow that. Dover suffered from that frenetic type of person that believed the next place was where they needed to be. Quickly. Cars whizzed.

All of a sudden we were beyond the suburbs. Bright celandine and subtle violets along a cycle path told us. The cars became occasional but they still whizzed.

Villages emerged, as did the spaces between them. A sense of a good trek crept over us. Hey, we were doing it and it felt pretty endomorphic-rush brilliant.

Hills came into the equation. No surprise, really, as the railway journey gave us a good idea of the immediate topography. Our train had passed above Dover marina as we peered disappointedly across the sea to glimpse France through the haze, yet Dover Castle was seen high on the famous white cliffs. The craning of our necks had told us we were going to witness hills.

Cathy's first day of jogging

It took a while but, about 4 miles in, we were breaking into a sweat going up them. Cathy's jog and my cycling had turned to a walk whenever we met anything steep. Lydden proudly heralded their title of Best Kept Kent Village and, in our view, lived up to its nomenclature with the only blemish being the parking around the school. There is a modern mania of fearful parents and even grandparents who take a car to a primary school when the healthy option is available. Lydden, like so many rural lower schools had good pavements for the surrounding quarter of a mile, so, even cars carrying outlaying pupils could be parked a good way from their classrooms and have a healthy walk in and out. Those driving within that distance also clearly lack the understanding of what constitutes a healthy option. Nobody can be always short of time. Then comes the type that want to show off a new BMW, all at the expense of the child's long-term physical well-being. Furthermore, who can smell violets, or hear a warbler from a Mercedes?

Did someone get me started?

As I was struggling on my bike, up the hill into Shepherdswell, a local cyclist commented, "Those panniers look heavy, any gold bars?" Little did I realise at the time, but he had provided an excuse I was to use many-times-over during the coming weeks. Cathy jogged up to join our conversation of pleasantries with the man as I extracted his directions to the local station. From a late afternoon start and after a long train journey, that was enough for the day so Cathy was congratulated while the man held her in awe at what she looked to achieve. I was just carrying the gold bars.

Our recently formed plan was to stop at Shepherdswell, one of he few villages on the railway line, in order to take the train to Canterbury YHA (Youth Hostel Assn.), then return by train to resume from where we finished this day. It was all legal. No inches were ever gained.

We arrived at Shepherdwell Station on the wrong platform. A large wooden bridge was our only route to the Canterbury-side. The weight of our heavy touring bike, fully laden with full panniers formed a daunting task, which would test the two of us. Suddenly a lady I can only describe as a white Nicola Adams (UK's Olympic power-packed boxer) ran over the bridge, grabbed the bike, lifting it high into the air, then jogged (dare I say manfully?) up the steps, along the parapet and down the other flight and onto the correct platform, just in time for the correct train. Magical! Pity she was not around at Canterbury!

We found the Canterbury YHA despite local knowledge. We spent some time laughing about my slow motion fall from the bike as I tried to stop during our trek. How many of those were to come?

We relaxed into the lovely facilities of the hostel, then pizza and beers or wine all helped us to bed. Ooooh! Bed!

That was:

Dover-Temple Ewell-Lydden-Coldred-Shepherdwell

On-course Miles: 6.5. Day's total: 9

Sat 25th March From Shepherdswell

Quite simply, the best ever journey we have ever taken in Kent.

Mind, it began with a train guard throwing my bike around just because it stuck out into the aisle by 3 inches as we got back to our restart. He ran away. I think he shrank from being pierced by Cathy's eyes more than my shouting.

From sunny Shepherdswell station (where there was no need for the bridge, thankfully), we soon found the National Cycle Route (CR) 16, which was to be our friend all the way to Canterbury. Dog violets and celandine lined almost all the charming way, with wood anemones in one glade.

Our summation that primroses do not fare well on chalk was justified by their complete absence but we were not sure of our facts. (A lack of facts has never stopped me from holding an opinion, so why start now?). *Later research proved me wrong of course.*

As we set off that morning, a local directed us to "cross the level crossing…" We cursed her stupidity as we had just left the train in the valley and the Dover line was clearly marked on our map. What our map did NOT have marked was The Kent South Downs Steam Railway line! Curse reversed.

We were soon on open rural roads that could be seen stretching almost to a vanishing point while welcomed wooded areas sheltered us from the fierce easterly winds. I cycled excitedly down a lane that cut through one of these woodlands, full of glee. When the woodland ended, I was exposed to a near-head-on wind that filled my anorak and turned it into a parachute, with the same affect as the one on a drag-car. I almost felt pushed backwards going downhill!

Cathy's pace was more of a constant plod, yet remarkable to appreciate. We took more time in the villages, all of which appeared pretty. Barfrestone had a white-stoned 12th Century church with ornate carvings that shone in the sun. Aylesham had a triangular village green with daffodils trumpeting towards the red and grey church across the meadow. Here we saw a shutdown pub. "Been shut for 10 years, mate. It gets knocked down on Tuesday." We were told.

"Anywhere here serving Coffee?" We pleaded.

"No, you have just missed the church hall charity morning."

The village was a mile long, probably consisting of 500 houses, yet no shop or tearoom and no competing large town for 10 miles. Perhaps it was due to the lack of through-trade, but the next lady, walking her dog at the far end of the village, blamed the commuters. Just then, as if on cue, the first fast car of the day swung round the tight corner of the lane. "They will hit a horse one day, they don't understand the countryside," she said, and then off she toddled.

Vitamin D blazed on our cheeks as we settled for a banana each and a shared orange on the roadside verge. Getting down to sit created just as many creaks as when we rose. Cathy's knee was holding up today. Its swollen cartilage had caused a twinge yesterday, so she took no risks and this had paid off. After yesterday's run/walk she feared for aches and pains that had, thankfully not appeared.

As we passed a herd of cattle, I told Cathy they blow one up to get more money. The explosion makes a caldera (cow dearer). Sorry. The geography teacher got it. Eventually.

Beyond Aylesham, keen buzzards kee-eu'd high on the early-year thermals and a mile further on, skylarks practised their choruses. Then, on two separate occasions, a brimstone butterfly passed us at nostril height. It just went to show us that, even in March, our countryside can yield natural wonders.

We cycled/jogged past the oast houses of Patrixbourne, then survived 20 yards of the A2 before snaking off and up a farmer's lane. It felt like an old drover's lane, you could sense the history through high-bank configurations and gnarled trees. We realised its true identity when, after 2 miles, it was signposted as Watling Street, the Roman-paved track used by ancient Britons. A further 1¾ miles on, we could see the upper features of Canterbury Cathedral. As we took in the panorama we realised we had not seen a human or vehicle for the last hour and a half, then celebrated the fact.

The track then descended into a suburb, Barton, which led us to the New Dover Road, a two-mile avenue with

our hostel somewhere along it. Fortunately for us, it turned out to be just another 150 yards. On that last corner stood a local Post Office, the only shop we saw on our day's journey! A telling factor of modern village life. **That was:**
Shepherswell-Barfrestone-Aylesham-Adisham-Patrixbourne-Barton-Canterbury 11 Miles

Sunday March 26th From Canterbury

Good job I was wearing cycling shorts under my tracksters as I carried the two panniers down the flights of grand stairs in our YHA. At the top, the pin holding my tracksters up (the elastic was long gone) popped. By the time I reached base camp they were round my knees. I waddled like a penguin.

From east of Canterbury we were always going to need to go through or round the city. The experiences previously have led us to believe that towns do not work on long treks yet this one did. Partly driven by the need for elastic, we passed through its thriving epicentre with fine, old architecture and pleasant folk, some curious of our plight (especially when re-threading the elastic in a removed pair of tracksters).

We passed through the ancient gate on Watling Street and then climbed, almost unnoticeably, up the outlying ridge to the north. We found grasslands and trees where the first blackcap was heard. He probably over winters here these days, it saves the airfare.

Canterbury Cathedral's spires settled 100ft below our viewpoint as Kent College boys played on the school grounds behind us.

I ask you, dear reader, if there is any more-twee name for a long path than the "Crab and Winkle Line'? It followed the old railway track from Canterbury to Whitstable, cutting through grand woodland and areas of arable acreage. It began alongside the noisiest vineyard we have ever seen. Polythene covers, high on stilts fluttered in the strong easterly. Forestry had been established long enough to form topsoil for primroses or were we now out of the chalky downs? *Cathy's correction: we were still in them!*

Cathy ran using a protective stride, not daring to overstretch her cartilage. I just loved cycling beside her, even at walking pace. This did need a technique I am not fully familiar with. I had perfected the tear-at-it approach in my earlier life but now; hey, slow is cool. However, I tore off down a long hill out from the woodland with enough momentum to glide up the corresponding rise at the far side. This took me over the dual carriageway of the A2. I stopped there for Cathy when a passing walker said, looking down at the cars, "Crazy, aren't they?" I agreed yet Cathy had her own slant on it. "Better," she said, "To have a single corridor of madness so this place," she waved her arm over the unspoilt countryside, "is free." I am not one to disagree with her when she is so forceful.

So, 10 miles in and we smelt the outskirts of Whitstable. An old man in voluminous khaki shorts wandered ahead of us on a cycle lane at the back of a housing estate. Some 70 yards ahead of us he stepped sharply left into the bushes. "*Please, please let him be a flasher.*" I thought. As I approached, there in the gap, I realised it was his back gate.

The first railway bridge of the day stood above and near us. Cathy stopped suddenly to read a direction sign partially obscured by a tree. Inexplicably, her knee went, it was likely to have been her inflamed cartilage, we suspected. She could not move and was desperate. She

17

cried, partly through pain but mainly due to her undying wish for fairness. "I've ruined it for you," she said dejectedly. My placations and looking on the bright side views were orchestrated in the narrow slits of hope. We could both see the end of our long trek ending there, on a lane in Tankerton. For 10 minutes Cathy could not move. For another 10 she attempted to stand and 5 more went by as she learnt to hobble using walking poles. She felt me being very supportive, but I knew how wonderful she had been near Kirkintillock on our Lands End to John O'Groats walk, when I ricked my back. The shoe was now on the other knee.

Whitstable's 1970's housing estates were not exactly cheering us on but we eventually limped on and found the High Street after an hour of struggling. Our bike and panniers were padlocked to the drainpipe outside the café as we cleared a large pot of tea and cakes whilst being entertained by broods of children totally in control of their parents.

Throngs on the High Street this weekend were like an un-crossable river. At the newsagents, I parked the bike on its stand in the kerb-side, and then faced the shop's door, three feet away. Families from the right, teenagers from the left, followed by an oblivious texter, then two girls deep in chat-mode. I had stood for two minutes without a hint of a gap in either direction from the two-way human traffic. Action was needed. My florescent yellow anorak'ed arm flew up swiftly, the left one pointed out straight, brushing the nasal hair of a pedestrian and, like Moses, I parted the ways, Shocked folk stood aghast at the newsagent's door. Close behind me, I could hear Cathy's giggle.

We had booked a B&B in Seasalter, a good 2 miles out of town. Off Cathy hobbled, soon finding the seawall. The CR 1 recommended a left turn inland but we were told the sea-wall route took us in the direction of Seasalter. We should not have laughed but we did when, at the end of the sea wall, we faced a series of old wooden groynes stretching as far as the eye could see. Each entailed a lifting of the bike, laden with panniers. Up, bump, rumble (over pebble beach) up, bump, rumble harmonised with hobble, hobble up, ouch, hobble, hobble from Cathy. Release came after 400 yards in the form of the appropriately named Joy Lane that became the Faversham Road and house No1. Our B&B was No. 230. On our way, we called into the Oyster Pearl pub who told us "Food finishes at 5-30 and we are fully booked". Strangely enough, we returned at 10 past 5 to watch England win 2-0 against Lithuania and were served willingly with roast beef. The reason we had to watch soccer in a pub was our £100 per night B&B did not have terrestrial TV. "We would have to buy 3 TV licences if we did that", Jez said. At £100 a night, he should soon afford it.

A careful night's rest for Cathy's knee.

That was: Canterbury-Tankerton-Whitstable-Seasalter 11 miles

Mon March 27th From Seasalter

Cloud had capped our world and distant mist was a feature. Cathy's knee was hoping to book out of our makeshift intensive care unit. Over breakfast, Cathy suggested reversing the roles after she road-tested her knee on the bike. Plans were disrupted by a photo-shoot by Jez outside their B&B for their Facebook images and promotional output.

In the end, Cathy did the walking. She began poorly then improved over the last mile. We just had to make it to a reasonably sized town to get a decent diagnosis, and then the appropriate help (or surrender). For my part, I pushed the bike most of the way. The first few miles were on the main coastal road. It was not busy, but the cars had no reason to be slow, so it was far from pleasant, but it was direct. We needed to hit a town to see what we could do next.

This part of Kent had little to soothe us. The marshland was more scruffy than scenic and the mudflats or seawalls were equal in their sterility.

Beyond Graveney church, CR 1 turned right, down a dead end lane, onto the marshes along to a well-formed path. The greater tranquillity enabled us to hear and see a charm of goldfinches as well as a host of birdsong. I once knew the difference between sedge and reed warblers' calls but I realised I now know no more. At least I knew it was one of them.

We almost celebrated the road to the sewage works just because it was flat, a boon to Cathy's leg as we walked into Faversham. This raised our hopes on continuing tomorrow, if not a delight to our noses. Faversham church had been a steeple in the distant mist for most of the morning yet there it was directly above us. Shepherd Neame, UK's oldest continuous brewery, was close to cater for the other type of religion. The quaintness of the town, and that of our newly found B&B, drew us in.

This was a short day that could well have ended with a homeward train, but Cathy's powers of recovery meant we would fight another day. Having worn a hole through her running shoes, she went off to the shops for more.

That was: Seasalter-Graveney (batsman Tom must have hailed from this hamlet)-Thames Marshes-Faversham   7.1 miles

Tues March 28th From Faversham

Mary, our fine overnight B&B host, was Irish, yet Cathy wondered if she and I were related, given two main reasons:

Firstly, she had asked last night what we would like for breakfast and we all agreed that scrambled eggs and smoked salmon would be lovely and convenient. Then, at the breakfast table, two plates were delivered with a fried egg on each. Cathy eyed me and humped her shoulders. Bacon followed, then sausages, "oh, nice small roast potatoes," beans then, with a flourish, mushrooms! Another look, another shrug.

Secondly, her cardigan was inside out. I did not notice this. Nor, until we had cycled for two hours, did I notice my cycling shorts proudly displayed my padded linen crutch on the outside!

You may have noticed the "we cycled" bit. Last night, Cathy went to a physio, slapped prescribed cream on her knee and applied a prescribed ice pack on it. The same ice pack that remained within Mary's freezer, never to be seen again. This morning, the knee was not playing ball and socket. So, we bought a bike. Yes, it surprised us, too. As a consequence, our departure was delayed while Mr Bike Warehouse set up the seat and the handlebars. We wandered off for a coffee (now I know why that lady looked amazed at me, Mr InsideOut when I left the loo), then collected the bike to rejoin the CR1. Having re-joined it, we soon left it again unintentionally. If this was to be the first time we got lost, it surely would not be our last. CR1 was only found after a few scary moments on the A2. We vowed to avoid those skirmishes with half-ton, speedy killers, let alone the 30 ton ones.

Soon, the chiffchaffs lined the way, as cars were unseen while newly leaved copses gleamed. Cathy was getting used to her new bike, the expense of which she had justified because the number of nights' lodgings would be reduced by taking less days for the journey. It was beautiful to be pedalling together through soft-fruit farms and at least one natural burial ground around the ancient orchards.

A seawater creek came in at Conyer where we found The Ship Inn. We lapped up lime & sodas at the ship-lapped Ship. It was nestled next to winter-stored yachts and barges, hidden from the ravages of weather and from the eyes of owners only interested in fair-weather sailing. This bright, warm March day made a mockery of their incarceration while justifying our thirst-quencher, enhanced by a ploughman's lunch. I never did see the ploughman. Bet he was annoyed.

Almost immediately, the acquaintance of both green and greater spotted woodpeckers was lost and oystercatchers befriended us. Wide expanses of inland sea covered the panorama as we cycled atop the sea-bank high above the brine to our right and the sedge on the landside to our left.

Curiously, Kent Council (who maintain these fine cycle paths) had installed slender metal gates and high stiles within them that almost eliminate any continuous long distant cycling. The contortions for a bike with panniers would be beyond many folk without taking the bag carriers off and reloading after every one. I yelled my intolerance, "Kent Councils: which word of Long-Distance Cycle Paths do you not understand?" Cursing helped me grit my teeth as I pushed head-on into a south westerly.

Back into farmland, we found a twisted signpost. This was not an unusual occurrence when locals do not fancy intrusion, but still annoying. We made the correct decision there, but missed a further sign (or it may have been sabotaged). Over the hill and far away, we went, eventually finding a railway we were not supposed to find. Lost, we were. Back to the nearest farm, the bare-chested hunk of rural Heathcliff sent us down his private lane with his blessing. We found the railway crossing he mentioned where the gates were being upgraded to solar propulsion. Progress for the rail network, I guessed but not necessarily for two lost travellers who had strayed from their tracer-bullet path. We were only marginally less lost than when we were certain of being lost. Then came Sittingbourne.

It would be tedious to discuss the last 3 miles because it involved Sittingbourne, a settlement that personified tedium. Add lashings of anguish, too.

Trying to find decent food was a case in point. I considered all the local eating establishments, checked reviews on Trip Advisor, then swept Cathy off her feet to take her where you could find the finest food in town: Tesco Express. Really, the options were that shocking. Our own hotel was 4 star (it said) without a restaurant. It was run by a man who had greeted us wearing a dirty blue T-shirt proclaiming, "I am not fat, I'm kidnap protected." Any trace of humour was lost in our Tesco wraps.

That was: Faversham-Conyer-Tong Mill-Sittingbourn 10 miles but 3 extra getting lost

Wed March 29th From Sittingbourne

Overnight traffic was not 4 star, either and the hotel's egg on toast had all the culinary delights of cardboard. This was a day of happy grumbles. Cathy gave instructions that my blood pressure should not be compromised, so I laughed whenever I grumbled. Old farts need to grumble, don't we?

Last night's (Cathy's) devious route planning gave us a direct way back to C.R.1 with a few swerves around the north eastern edge of Sittingbourne. "The quicker we leave Sittingbourne, the better," I grumbled. Later that morning, a friendly cyclist was to agree with me. A polite, well-spoken man yet liberal enough to use the word "Sh**hole". He was also the first person so far to read our notice and say he knew where Cape Wrath was.

The now-familiar orchards, mainly young orchards, lined our way with poly-tunnels beginning to proliferate. Old caravans (huddled round like wild-west wagons as the Apaches approached) were another common feature, providing homes for the populations of migrant workers. The topography of the lanes became more undulating, a feature that became the norm for the day. This was contrary to the overview given that we were travelling along the coast and riversides. We came into Rainham's Country Park, much of it hewn from old cement quarrying. This municipal sporty facility clearly helped upgrade the cycle route but, yet again, Kent's wonderful authorities had installed large blocking contraptions that force cyclist to dismount, twist the bike and squeeze any panniers through metal bars. Thus, by providing cycling lanes for cycling, they halted cycling every few yards so we had to engage in contortions and swearing. On this day, we would say me must have seen 25 of these monstrosities. How dumb do they want us to look?

My agonised senses were tickled back to happiness by the blackthorn and alexanders lining the way to the mudflats of the Medway Estuary. There, above the salted mud-blanket stood a wooded island with the glorious name of Horrid Hill. After a mile or two, we turned inland, parallel to the Medway River. From here on, it seemed, we were in an industrial estate with major roads running through it. This was unavoidable as all routes funnelled to the first inland road-bridge over the major river Medway. Gillingham, Rochester and Chatham blurred into one leading to a crescendo of fear when crossing the darn thing on an unprotected cycle lane. The strong westerly wind pushed us towards the lorries in the next lane, so Cathy got off and walked the last part.

Lunch nearby eased our nerves and found a gem for our eyes. The Ship Inn (yes, another one) overlooked Chatham Docks and in the lagoon sat a Russian submarine from World War II. An unusual sight that is now used for film scenes, we were told.

Chalk cliffs lined the river, so we had a steep incline followed by a respective decline, which mirrored the ups and downs of this busy world. Flatness arrived as a cycle track turned into a Thames-side gravel lane with an old, disused canal on our left and the high bank of the Thames on our right. Bums bounced and yells were emitted, but we got along the 2-or-3 mile stretch to Gravesend. The Clarendon Royal hotel gave us a cheap deal and high cuisine, so the complaints were appeased. It was a delightful evening but, after our longest day yet, we were truly knackered.

That was:
Sittingbourne-Rainham-Gillingham-Rochester-Chatham-Church Street-Gravesend
22 miles

Thurs 29th March From Gravesend

We knew there would be plenty of rubbish to get through on this leg but, boy, did we experience it. I guess we should blame the modern world for the 6-lane era of thundering lorries and white-van-man-meets-Formula One mentality. If one word sums it up it is 'urgency', but that does not capture the noise. I guess we all contribute, but it was not good to experience it on a bike.

Eggs Royale had started the day off so deliciously but we had to hold onto that taste as dust and debris were splattered at us by passing 44 tonners. We had to cycle 4 miles inland on the (not very close to the river) "Thames Path" due to a few industrial and military edifices on the actual waterway. Bluewater and Ebsfleet International were also navigational bollards, each of several hundred acres.
After all this, Dartford town was a doddle. Weaving through housing estates led us to a narrow footbridge over lorries queuing for their Dartford Tunnel crossing.

The Darent River became our next conquest. Having crossed it inland, we rode a narrow, stony track above its muddy flanks exposed at low tide. The first swallow of the year flew along helping Cathy survive the bumpy 2-mile ride along the track. Then there was The Thames again after a round-route of 12 miles for us, to get back to the bank just 5 miles upstream..
It was narrow and at low tide waders were probing the mud. A redshank called. We were free again. It was a compressed mud surface that was wide enough to allow us to look up. London skyscrapers appeared just before lunch on lush grass in hot sunshine. Opposite, were the

hills of London's rubbish near Thurrock, some were old enough to be grassed over.

Our progression towards Inner London took us past the biggest scrapyard I could ever have imagined. They were crushing old cement-mixer lorries!

A spin inland due to the military firing range (they were firing as we passed) led us up to the café at the Thames Barrier. The till never worked in 2015 (our Thames Path walk) and nothing had improved in two years. We were hardly surprised. What did surprise us was the parks inability to consider cyclists due to so many flights of steps. Aaarrgghh!! Back onto the Thames Path proper, the surface was perfect but the barriers were not. I know I had moaned before, but this day gave us 43 sets of encumbrances, some only 10 yards apart!! Just how much Granny-killing speed could I generate in 10 yards? I hit several steel bars. Not accidently, but with my clenched hand. Oh, and a couple of sticks.

Going mad at stiles (Jackie Charlton once did that)

We cycled the complete peninsular of the O2 Arena. Not that we meant to, but it was a nice day. Well, it stopped being nice on the far, upstream side when a diversion stopped us progressing and took us back across the peninsular and dumped us in a busy street near North Greenwich. Happiness dwindled swiftly close to the end of our sweaty day. Local folk got us back to Greenwich College where we parted the crowds to find our B&B. Our part-time Londoners and dear friends, Cousin Richard and his wife Fern came for dinner. We did not eat either of them.

That was:
Gravesend-Dartford-Bexley-Thames Barrier-O$_2$ Arena-Greenwich 32 miles

O2 Arena across The Thames

FRIDAY 31st MARCH From Greenwich

Cycling under The River Thames was a weird concept. On this day, we did just that at the Greenwich Foot Tunnel. Yeah, I know it says no cycling, but everyone did it.

We paid for our misdemeanour on The Isle of Dogs. The Cycle Route 1 headed straight on. The map showed it wiggled through housing estates along the west edge from where we would have to cut back to the east, so why not stay and follow the Thames Path (North bank)! So we made our mistake, not obviously, by gliding along the river but then we were shoved into Millwall's housing estates. Glimpses of the land adjoining the river could be seen. One was through a private estate with a man in a yellow box who said, "Yes you can get out along a walkway here, go ahead". Sure enough, we could go along it. Sure enough it was only 27 yards long. Dejected, we pedalled on.

Our intention was to follow the River Lea's towpath northwards. However, nobody we asked knew where The River Lea was. Some could not speak English; a couple of dodgy ones just kept their heads down providing nothing, not even a murmur and walked on. "*Probably illegal immigrants*" we thought. "*Or anti-cyclist activists*", yet, more than likely, just deaf like me. Then, the posh offices appeared of The Canals and River Trust. Cathy got through the electronically locked gates and found the man in charge. He had not heard of The Lea, a river within a mile of his classy abode and could not find it in his computer system. Now if Cathy, a Geography Teacher, knew nothing about Geography, I wonder how long she would have lasted in her job? Having had much experience of Government quangos and having known those who wangle their way onto them, I can assure the uninitiated that quangos have never shown any ability to do anything. Furthermore, some were formed to make sure nothing was done. (Heavily-influenced-by-my-past) rant over.

This disappointment of ignorance was extenuated when Cathy was locked-in behind the compound's electric gates. The intercom to the office was on the other side of the gates and tantalisingly out of reach to her. Somebody had not planned for this (highly likely) situation. It was only luck that I heard her yells above the noise of Canning Town's traffic before getting the inmates to realise they had effectively imprisoned my wife against her will.

We found "The Lea Valley Walkway" and "The Lea Riverhead" and followed the signs that led us northwards along the waterway. We thought we had cracked it! The path of the creek at low-tide lifted us onto a bridge as the river became tightly bunded between high walls. We expected to rejoin it shortly on the other side, but life in busy London did not work like that. God knows why they called the short stretch a "Valley Walkway". The Lea had vanished. As its replacement, the strangled streets of Canning Town did not fit the bill. Outside Star Lane's underground station, all hell had industrially broken loose. Huge articulated lorries reversed; others lined up to pass; diggers drilled through concrete; abandoned cars with no tyres lined the roadside; broken glass from smashed windscreens was laying everywhere. We were lost and, in the process, we were becoming terrified.
One escape route was blocked by a business's private estate, gated and secured, so we had to double-back. We

found a main road, heading towards the Olympic Park's "helter-skelter." While on this, Cathy spotted the elevated cycle route to the park. That haven was created to avoid the thunderous traffic; it was a delight to cycle.

In the Olympic Park, we asked four policemen for directions to the River Lea. Despite the river being less than a quarter of a mile from the spot, none of the policemen knew where it was. They knew where the café was. They suggested local information might reside there, not with them.

The café was inside the Aquatic Centre, so we made our first-ever visit within. The coffee was good, the information was non-existent. We found a map and a bike-lift up to the upper bridges. Inside the lift, we wedged our bikes against the back wall, pressed buttons and the lift rose. Once the lift stopped, we stared at the doors that had just closed in anticipation of them opening and heard the usual drawing apart of metallic equipment. Sadly, this did not come from the doors we were staring at but came from behind us. We turned to see, beyond our bank of cycles, the opening to an upper-floor space, which we craved but could not reach. The button to keep the doors open was beyond two handlebars and a gear changer or two. A fingertip brushed it just as the doors were closing in on us. The contortion of us turning one bike to get to another was Mr Bean-like. By stretching across one bike to jiggle a second one into the opening we just made it (after the doors closed on us twice). Houdini would have been proud.

Up high, we went over the Water Works inlet and, beyond and below The Olympic Stadium, we found The River Lea. The S-slope slid us down but there, between two high bridges, was a "Kier Construction PLC" building site stopping us going further on either bank. There was no way upstream, Cathy had seen a sign pointing downstream to Hackney Wick, I said downstream was London, Hackney Wick should be north. A desperately low point. We squabbled a bit more; just to make sure we were truly getting nowhere. Strangely, "nowhere" can be broken into "now here"! About right!

A cycling form of retreat took us back up over the bridges and onto a major main road where we found a local man of Indian descent who became our most helpful person to date. Triumphantly, we trundled down Copper Street and onto a gorgeous surface of The Lee Navigation Cycle Path (note the subtle, and defining change of spelling from River Lea to Lee Navigation). Back came the Health & Safety barriers in various shapes and forms, courtesy of Hackney Borough Council, requiring dismounts, waddles and pannier-juggling. Cathy's nerves were tested with the sheer drops to the river on offer but she stood the test. We were soon tanking along.

By 2.30pm, the sun came out and the southerly wind was helpfully on our backs. Skimming past my old fishing haunts of Dobb's Weir and Field's Weir kept me more engaged than Cathy. My constant commentary of every gudgeon I had ever caught may have dragged on a bit for My Lovely. I was surprised she stayed awake. From Eastwick into Harlow, there was not an inch I had not fished. Boy, I must have been boring!

The day had seen our longest section yet; close to 40 miles, but it had taken 7½ hours! In Harlow, an enjoyable evening with my darling sister, Julie and her perfect hubby, Tony sorted us out.

Some very interesting gudgeon caught here in 1967

That was: Greenwich-Milwall-Isle of Dogs-Canning Town-Olympic Stadia of Stratford-Hackney Marshes-Waltham Abbey-Cheshunt-Broxbourne-Hoddesdon-Glen Faber (no longer exists)-Roydon-Little Parndon-Harlow 37miles

Sat April 1st. From Harlow

With those niggly bits of bacon lodged firmly in our teeth for full-day irritation, we set off from the waving Bondeanos, Julie and Tony, and their love-rich home. I wished our own love would have kept untarnished all day, but a rutty towpath ruined that. All was fine up to The Old Mill at Old Harlow Lock. The surface up to then had been laid as part of the 2012 Olympic infrastructure, but it stopped there. Rather like our happiness. We discussed the best way to Bishop's Stortford from that point in an area we both knew well. Cathy had previously made an analysis of Sustrans' maps for

cycling routes, cross-checked with Google Maps and verified contours on Ordnance Survey maps. She suggested a lane route. I checked the mud ahead and returned with the bad news that the miles of nice riverside cycle paths had stopped along my preferred route. Cathy asked, "Now, which way would YOU go?"
"The" ("my"), "River, but…" (I never got to say what I thought we SHOULD do)
"Okay," moaned Cathy, "we will go the river way. That's it!!"
Martyrdom is a dire sport; it has seen some good, saintly folk suffer pain they ill deserved. This was Cathy's turn. If there had been a wooden cross handy, she would have nailed 3 of her limbs to the wood, then passed the hammer to me to tack the final hand. A very low point.

In that area, we were in familiar territory but it had been 40 years since the back of our hands could be used as reference. This was despite my bristling pride that I THOUGHT I knew the way. Our backs had eventually been turned on The River Stort at Sawbridgeworth in favour of the lanes of Hallingbury and a happier married life. By the time we saw The Stort again it was a small stream in the illustratively named Bishop's Stortford. My cricketing days came flooding back as we on-drove into gentle North Essex. Cathy could hardly wait for the tales. There was Farnham, where Hot Chocolate's guitarist, Tony Wilson played alongside his batsman son, Felix. Manuden next, where our son-in-law's cousin, Brett stopped us to compare notes with his 2,000 mile epic cycle of The USA.

Back lanes took us peacefully up the ridge to a bench on Rickling Green where I bored Cathy with the tale of a passing mini whose radiator I caved in with a rare well-timed off-drive. The driver was kind enough to take the blame for stopping to watch and, sitting there looking over the green to The Cricketer's Arms, you could see why he would have taken time to appreciate the view.

The tranquil, pre-season scene gave us space for some reckoning. It was to be a further 26 miles to Cambridge, which would be pushing ourselves. Our contemplation brought my forthcoming brain surgery on April 6th into focus. Yeah, it shocked us, too. We had already set April 2nd as the latest we could get back home for the pre-op bits and Cambridge was beyond where we hoped to have reached, but it gave us a good train network to get back home.

We decided to press on and allow the afternoon to evolve. From the plains of Rickling, we found the western tip of Clavering just after a merlin had flown alongside Cathy down the hill: the bird, not the successful World War II aircraft.

It was 2pm at The Cricketers yet we still stopped for two starters from the appealing menu. These were so yummy, we stayed the night in order to enjoy an a la carte dinner and turn on the romance.

This was a chance to live it up on a good deal and, yet again, subject poor Cathy to cricketing tales. The pub / restaurant had long been the home of Keith Oliver and his wife, now more widely known as Jamie's parents. Keith was probably the best-dressed cricketer in village cricket. The buckskin pads always saw more of the ball than his bat, but what a fine host. Jamie, as a youngster seemed more forced into the team than selected and has subsequently shown his talents to lay elsewhere. It was time to forget the charming thatched-roof pavilion overlooking the sloping pitch and turn to my lovely wife over a fine Oliver meal.

That was Harlow-Sawbridgeworth-Little & Great Hallingbury-Bishop's Stortford-Farnham-Manuden-Rickling Green-Claveering
25 miles

Sunday, April 2nd From Clavering

Okay, the stay was a tad extravagant but worth every penny. Our breakfast of fine cuisine set us up to seek the back-lanes towards Cambridgeshire. The very next village was Arksden and its quaint pub, The Axe and Compass. This was the regular (and last) drinking hole of Steve Marriot of The Small Faces. My old pal, Richard Smith tended to keep him company, and did so on the last night, as Steve loved an audience. Steve's wife was away, taking their daughter to a school in Manchester. So there was Steve, fresh from L.A.. He was buzzing on more than just jetlag and talking to Richard of his next venture. He continued to do so as Richard kept with him all the way to his gate at the end of the night. Steve's candle was never extinguished until the roof of his house-by-the-church went up. His body was found in the wardrobe. Wrong exit, Steve. All or Nothing?

Blazing, yes appropriately, blazing sunshine glazed our path past the very house and onto even more minor roads through Littlebury Green and Catmere End. Herds of MAMILS were out (Middle Aged Men In Lycra), utilising the best Sunday morning so far this year. Over the last major ridge, just south of Ickleton, we had a panorama that stretched over Cambridge with knowledge of flat Fenlands were waiting for us somewhere out there. Geographic historians say The Thames reached the sea at Ipswich some 450,000 years ago, prior to breaking through the Chilterns at Goring

36

Gap. When you see the slope in Ickleton, you may wonder if it was once a Thames Southbank.

At Duxford, an antique aircraft flew over us as we headed to Whittlesford where, at The Tickle Arms, the famous queen Kim De La Taste Tickle (R.I.P.) once held sway over his squire-dom. He holds the distinction of being the only landlord to throw me out of a pub whilst in the company of a Lord of the Realm. A feat never likely to be repeated.

Blackthorn hedge and Cathy's style

The young River Cam between Whittlesford and Sawston once saw Minimus Jack rescue me from a freezing current on a boozy fishing trip. Appropriately, our song, entitled, "While Away" has the lines:
"On the bank, glass on hand,
Any old drink, any old brand'"...

Jack dutifully stripped, regardless of the snow, to lend me his long-Johns (well, barely "short"-Johns). Both human and fishing tackle were displayed without our knowledge of the walking party passing by until we heard the applause.

We only skirted Sawston, a small town south of the expanding city of Cambridge. CR11 had been designed to virtually bypass Sawston intentionally. It did not mean to bypass Cambridge itself but our failure to spot one of the signs meant we nearly did circumnavigate the whole of the conurbation of Cambridge.

As we drifted past Addenbrookes's Hospital from the Cherry Hinton area (yes, how did we get over there?), we found that everyone seemed to be cycling.

We realigned our sights and headed for Cambridge Station on the basis that train services ran to our village via Ipswich. Sadly, when I checked for engineering works disruptions, I had done so for yesterday (before our unplanned stop at Clavering). Today, we were faced with a rail replacement Bus Service. Aaaarrrggghh! With bikes! Aaaarrrggghh!

Now, Cathy and I have travelled on trains in many parts of the world. The best, finest and regular are the British...... at Bus Replacements.

There were a few panics, I admit, but the coach driver allowed me to slide the bikes into the luggage "belly" of the coach, then off we sent to Ely. By boarding a train there, changing at Ipswich and Mark's Tey then alighting at Chappel & Wakes Colne, we learnt a great deal about bike storage on the very varied trains of The Greater Anglia Network.

So, this is the break. They review me on Tuesday, cut me on Thursday 6ᵗʰ April. If I write any more, you can guess it went well.

That was:

Clavering-Arkesden-Littlebury Green-Catmere End-Ikleton-Duxford-Whittlesford-Sawston-Cambridge 25 miles

Tues 4th April: The operation's preview involved a few tests and a nurse who asked me if I was sure I wanted to go ahead. She made it plain; I could lose my sense of taste, either temporarily or for life. My sense of smell was in danger, too. As for the snipping bit, inside my head, well it was close to my optic nerve. A remote chance of blindness existed.

Cathy and I turned to each other and questioned whether this was a good idea to proceed. We trusted the surgeon and endocrinologist, so we agreed to the operation.

Thurs 6ᵗʰ Apr. The operation to remove a tumour from the edge of my brain.

Apr 9 I wrote a round-robin email to my friends and family:

Title: **Something On My Mind**

Dear sweet folks, even the slightly unsweetened ones, I am dearly indebted to those who made contact recently. It has meant a great deal to me and my wonderful wife, Cathy.

I have had something on my mind. Named "a Rathke Cleft Cyst," (*found later to be an adenoma*) this little fella has been growing on my pituitary gland (above and between the eyes) for many years, maybe from birth. It is possibly hereditary *(not)*. It sat in the lower regions of my brain. On Friday, this was removed by (fishing friends on Scilly will love this) Mr. Pollock, my neurosurgeon, by going up through my right nostril. Technically named a Transphenoidal Hypophysectomy; the operation took under three hours and I was out for 4. The cyst was drained and removed, leaving a cavity to be filled by either the pituitary gland or, more likely, cranial fluid. 48 hours later, I was watching The Grand National at home with Cathy, David & Sarah, followed by a lamb madras and a pint of Abbott Ale. Wonderful!

The experience of the operation can be described as going to the theatre, having some great drugs then waking up with a hole in my head and a broken nose. Just like a night out with Minimus Jack. I know we never took drugs, just alcohol, and the broken nose was the same one I went in with, but it cuts a great line.
So, in considering the small space currently in the lower brain, I can confidently declare there is, right now, nothing on my mind.
My kindest love to you all
Blind Boy Beard xxxxxx
Early April: Most of the time was spent making sure I was as fit as I thought I was, then running around to make sure everything was in place for our adventure. We had decided that both of us would cycle, using our hardy touring bikes and taking camping gear: tent, sleeping bags and mats. The preparation was both physical and mental.

Wednesday Apr 19 From (home, then) Cambridge

The wind was low but the spirits were high. Our dear friends, Katie and Siu had stayed over last night after a farewell meal in The Swan with David and Sarah Rayner. We were up and out an hour earlier than planned, so the chance to get an earlier train to Cambridge presented itself. We were too late to head to our village station to catch the local spur-line train, so we raced it to meet its mainline-connecting train to Ipswich. We made it.
You will recall that we left off at Cambridge, so that is where we needed to get back to. This involved getting two heavily laden bikes on and off trains; finding which end of each train they allow the things and the art of crushing innocent folks in inter-platform lifts. These just happened to be the low-points. The sights from the trains included the estuarine bliss of Manningtree and the thrill of Newmarket's gallops. Steady, Jim, I thought. Stay focussed. This adventure after such an operation is going to need concentration and endeavour.

First, it was coffee in Cambridge. This progressed to a Thai soup before we launched ourselves down Hills Road and into the heart of the fine city. Cathy looked rather flash in her new Laser cycling sunglasses as we avoided the Cambridge fleet of cyclists crossing Parker's Piece. Then, it was a bus that nearly wiped us out on the road before we reached the safe haven of Jesus Green. Thankfully, the driver's courtesy saved us and we were soon bankside of a sculling eight. I had tales to tell of this area, too, but, dear reader, you have suffered enough over the last 30 miles of what I can call, "My Manor".

41

The Cam by Jesus Green and our two tourers

CR 51 along The Cam in springtime is always worth attention and today was doubly so. I know Cathy was checking on my post-operation progress and I reckoned I was looking pretty darn good. Even so, the first few miles were taken at a gentle pace, just in case. Plus, due to the school holiday, I was more than capable of culling several of the dozens of playful small children. The calls of the rowing coach faded as our path headed away from the river yet we were still engaging with meadows and weeping willows. Seven miles in, and beyond Marshall's Cambridge Airport, was Bottisham. The large village gave us Magnum ice creams before we really deserved them. Only two more miles, beyond Lode (lode of jokes, there) was Fenland. A deep ditch on the side of the road signalled it, then WOW! The area began looking like The Somerset Levels before its unique character came through. It was hard to believe that its flatness could provide such beauty. Fortunately, cars could not use much of the tracks. I believed these ways to be old drovers roads that provided safe passage through the marshes of long ago. There were many loading blocks, too beside the tracks. They looked like the ranked podium of an Olympic medal ceremony but once the steps provided an easier approach to loading carts. Step up? Yes, talking of step up... We had a bad moment at the tall bridge over Wicken Fen. A chap with a light bike simply lifted his and trotted over. We had to dismantle all four panniers, carry them over, and then come back for each of the bikes to be double-handed up the unusually steep gradient of steps.

To lift us, our first 2017 dust storm spiralled upwards as we pressed onwards. Further compensation came at the National Trust tearooms when, perched on wires, there were swallows showing signs of migration fatigue.

We had been on CR1 from outside Lode and this beauty had taken us for a few miles down The River Ouse before entering Ely. Unlike the approach by road, the cathedral could only be seen during the last two miles. Summer madness had yet to hit the boating fraternity, so it was tranquil all the way to the centre of the city. Having elected to walk the bikes through the ancient streets, we were able to enjoy the architecture as well as a loving natter.

East Anglian accents had been first heard in The Fens and they flourished three miles on, in our resting spot for the night, Little Downham. Downham? I think I will, where's the pub?

Our new Vaude Lightweight tent was christened in the very peaceful Caravan Club site of Andy & Sylvia Meeks. They were free with the tea, biscuits and advice. The Plough Inn did the rest.

That was:
Cambridge-River Cam-Fen Ditton-Bottisham-Lode-White Fen-Wicken Fen-Adventurers' Fen-Ely-Little Downham 29 mile on course (33 miles in all)

Thurs Apr 20th From Little Downham

Our overnight warmth in the tent owed a lot to the clouds that accumulated, but the consequence was a day without sun. 2017's first night under canvas in April proved better for sleeping than many over-heated, over-priced bedrooms, so we were hearty. As was The Plough's breakfast.

Little Downham was a linear settlement; a long string of slender pearls for a mile, beyond which the farmland formed a flat desert of arable production on an industrial scale. A niggling southwesterly blew but our passage was so level we could not even call it a nuisance. Its influence was blocked entirely by the mighty 100 Foot Bank River. This is part of the drainage from Ouse Fen that once leaked its way to The Wash as part of The River Great Ouse system but was renamed The New Bedford River after the Duke and his investor-friends funded the bunding in exchange for vast areas of newly drained farmland. In one of nature's ironies, the hand-rubbing bankers (appropriate) watched the peat dry, crack and sink below the other rivers. It took the Dutch dyke-engineers to sort it out over a century later.
 By crossing this (New) river at Welney, the same road bridged The Old Bedford River and The River Delph. All

three are channels for that drainage of Ouse Fen to The Wash (together with the real Great Ouse to the east). The use of Old and New was relative. The masterworks for Old date from 1630 while the New was hardly modern, being completed in 1650. One could ponder how all this activity occurred during a Civil War.

Fen ditches in this region were often 10 feet below the road. Many were handsome waters, quite capable of sustaining roach and pike. Only 10% were affected by green algae.

By going through Welney and Christchurch, we had left CR11, picking our own way through the sporadic hamlets to find CR63. Long, straight roads appeared with their own vanishing point two or three miles into the distance. Many were named as Droves, relating to the days of droving livestock to the market towns. The cars were infrequent but two separate cars passed us at 100mph. That scared us!

Drizzle began just before Three Holes, driven on the southwesterly in a light veil. We sheltered near Laddus House in Laddus End (I imagined inside were beer-swilling pool players with jaeger bombs and dirty laughs). By the time we struggled into our waterproof trousers, there were only 17 specks of drizzle left.

Two further "drains" appeared alongside us on our steady cycle ride. The 16 Foot Drain was full to the brim at 20 feet across, then we crossed to The Middle Level Drain with its sweet, small lock at Marmont Priory with no sign of the priory. Perhaps it was prior to there.

There is a geographic theory that the nearer you get to the centre of a town, the older the buildings. Check it out and agree with Teacher Cathy. It certainly worked for Wisbech. In its market square, we found our hotel, The Rose and Crown, built in 1601. Strange, when you know we arrived in 14:32.

As we had finished early, we played tourists by visiting Peckover House. 1760 was when the Peckover family built their house on The Nene in town. Oddly enough, at 15:50, we walked round it, including the room used as a Quakers' bank in the family name, eventually selling out to Barclays. Now in the hands of The National Trust, it was a lovely Georgian Mansion.

Polish is not our first language; we can even struggle with English. So, popping into a Polski International shop was always going to be a laugh. I left the place not entirely sure if the cheese was not boiled goat's liver. Fortunately, Bryndza Podhalanska <u>was</u> cheese.

By checking the maps, we reckoned Wisbech was as far north as Birmingham. Things like that put some perspective on what we had achieved so far and cheered us. Did we need it? Well, sometimes.
That was: Little Downham-Pymoor (delicious name)-Welney-Tipps End-Christchurch-Three Holes-Upwell-Friday Bridge-Elm-Wisbech   25 miles

Fri Apr 21st From Wisbech

I thought Cathy had received an electric shock. She had stepped into the bath for a shower and, being aware that the first blast would be cold, she stepped to the rear of the bath. What she failed to notice was the angle of the showerhead. This was aimed directly at her new

46

position. With no possible retreat from the bath's rear, the cold blast hit her full on.

My morning story involved a lady parking roadside in the busy street while Cathy got the paper. Having parked quite reasonably, she looked up to see me watching. Seemingly self-consciously, she restarted her car, drove forward, reversed and made a complete hash of it. She drove forward again, reversed again, looked up at me, got out of the car for a look, got back in, drove forward and reversed. Finally happy, or beyond caring, she jumped out of the car, seemed to look for my approval and went on her way. "*Why oh why,*" I thought. Cathy came back and said, "With your fluorescent yellow cycling top, you look just like a copper!"

No sun again all day, so it was difficult to see which direction we were being taken by our chosen route. Mind you, the wind was a constant south-westerly, so we would have judged our direction every minute of the ride. I am sure we did not travel straight into it, but it was a darn nuisance.

Orchards proliferated on the land north of Wisbech, a surprise to us after being promoted yesterday by a fellow drinker predicting the delights of "The Apple and Orchard Project" in the area. Many old varieties, including 100 year-old Bramley trees exist with low-slung branches. The lack of livestock must be a benefit for the low fruit. The orchards' labour forces were a more recent addition to the area. I had not written of these matters earlier in fear of the political correctness Stasi, but their considerable contribution to our rural economy deserves a mention. When we saw a collection of steel, inter-continental containers in a huddle, we called them Bulgarian Housing Estates. Occasionally, they were formed of a small number of (not-so-) mobile homes in varying levels of dilapidation or clapped-out vans. These housed our erstwhile migrant workforce that ensure our British farmers can put food on our table at a price as reasonable as imports, whilst still making a profit despite excessive pressure from giant supermarkets.

I had written about the East Anglian twang heard in the region, but there were increasing numbers with Eastern European accents, even Baltic linguistic melodies. We even revelled in the delight of seeing a Latvian kebab van!

Quite separate from these settlements, were travellers' sites. These had steel gates (once belonging to someone else, perhaps), harsh lurchers, caravans, flash cars, huge, unmarked vans, a collection of coloured ponies and the obligatory heap of scrap metal en masse. We were told this species was known locally by its scientific name of *Pikii Gyppo*. It had taken root in several quarters of our travel off the beaten track and far from any constant eye.

Whilst clearing the air with honest reproach, I need to mention fly tipping. Blame was not thrown entirely at the travellers because signs of fast-food-eating townies and their penchant for lobbing aluminium cans into ditches must bear the brunt. The hundreds of items were there to stay, rotting to become an archaeological layer of our time in the peat.

The urban diet may have explained the high level of clinic obesity in the region's conurbations. The delineation came back to the accents. The trimmer figures were borne by those with the farm-workers' accent. The fatties were invariably indigenous.

Beyond the orchards were hectares of bulb-fields. Daffodils were dying, deliberately unpicked over mile upon mile of the bulb-producing field. These lined our route towards a couple of drains that ran to the North Sea as nameless waters on the OS maps, serving only to rid the land of moisture. In some cases, I will admit, they also served as ideal places for thriving fishing clubs.

We met The Welland's final few miles at Fosdyke Bridge. Here, another Ship Inn stood century to the A19 artery. We had planned to camp here but it was just too noisy. We were tired, but it was not going to work. The stop had allowed the use of the Internet and a bargain in a good hotel was discovered. So our tired limbs launched us back onto the pedals and a favourable wind launched us into quieter lanes towards Boston, 9 miles away. We had refound CR1, our metaphoric yellow brick road into the heart of the splendid market town and marina. The Stump (Boston's famous church tower) could be seen 4 miles out, yet ended only yards above our riverside hotel room at The White Hart.

Pizzaro, a 6-table Italian restaurant in the cobbled back streets brought back the romance despite two numb bums.

That was:
Wisbech-Tydd St Giles-Tydd St Mary-Fleet-Holbeach-Holbeach St Marks-Fosdyke Bridge-Frampton-Boston 36 miles (our longest since brain sergury?)

Sat 22nd April From Boston

Water birds became the main feature of the day: great crested grebes, coots, moorhens and kingfishers cheered us on our way along with tufted ducks, mallards, mute swans and messrs Greylag and Canada of the Goose Clan. We assumed the beefy locks at Boston on The Witham (locally pronounced With 'em) held back the freshwater from the sea and vice versa at high tide. The freshwater river was 70 yards wide at this point, harnessed between huge banks and straightened unnaturally. Once again, the work of long departed Dutch engineers still shapes our landscape.

34 miles of riverside cycling was on offer from Boston to Lincoln by The Water Rail Way, named after the shy water bird but with a nod to the old railway line that used to hug the southern bank. Maybugs and various flying insects flew in clouds around the hedges, many pinging off our cycling glasses and occasionally hitching a ride in an ear. Swallows would not be here without them, so forgiveness was on offer. So, too were the plumped-up swallows, resting on the wires after the morning's feast. So cute, virtually poetic.

Stating the obvious: the volume of water of the Witham, as with all rivers (not suffering from extraction), was greater at the sea. So, as we cycled upstream, often over in-coming sluices, we could see its earlier self, the streamline version. Like us all, looking back to our earlier days. 5 miles inland, it had been able to keep its natural meanders (me and 'er noticed), giving bends to add character. Particularly at the bends, the calm, sunny day allowed mirror reflections for our musing.

This was still CR1 but it sent us on a sabbatical to Holland Fen for probably the longest straight rural road of our entire journey. 7 miles bullet-straight, then just 15 yards of S-bend before a further 3 miles. There was no headwind, so it was a steady pedal-peddle.

Back on the riverside, we passed ghost railway stations with ceramic nameplates, like Stixwould on platforms that wait for the trains that will never arrive. Two miles outside Woodhall Spa, we were stopped in our tracks by a stunning piece of art. Sally Matthews's 'Lincoln Reds' and 'Lincoln Longwool Sheep' were metal and chain, yes, chains sculptures inspired by the poems of Alfred, Lord Tennyson and to commemorate the 200th anniversary of this former Poet Laureate who was born in Lincolnshire. They looked like real sheep crossing the path and were so lifelike we fed them grass.

Sally Matthews's flock

Woodhall Spa was passed almost unseen and we were away from settlements when a massive sugar refinery pushed us off the bank and into Bardney via a bridleway. The incumbent Heritage Centre of the large village housed Barry and his pictures of a local music festival of the late 60s. We saw the pictures and heard the tales of the Beach Boys wandering from pub to pub, stories that have made Barry what Barry was, is and always will be.

It was Barry who gave us a free place to pitch our tent on the side of the river. It was over rubble, round a gate and over the fence (hefty bikes included). Then a fight with the rabbits who seemed to own the space.

Our freshly cocked dinner at The Nag's Head was £4.95 each for the main course and £1 for homemade bread-and-butter pudding and custard. We are up North and loving it!!

That was:
Boston-River Witham-Holland Fen-Chapel Hill-Bardney 25 miles

Sun Apr 23rd From Bardney, Lincs.

The frost never hit us, so we woke from a snug night. Wild camping means a lot of nice things but breakfast is not included. Still, the day was still, so we needed to steel ourselves and steal a buttie somewhere.

Sunday racing cyclists were out in force. They sped past, yet those that spotted our notice wished us good luck. We hawked from village to charming village with the added interest of the first hills since North Essex. This did not suit my right groin, so we had three stops to give it a rest. During these breaks, we became the village entertainment either out of curiosity or in recognition of our madness. At The Bull Inn in South Kelsey there was a whole row of locals to pull our legs. They were quality jibes on account that each was a good long distance walker in their time, even the well-dressed Trish who sparkled. There were free pies on the bar on Sundays to compensate for the owners not cooking that day. That suited us, so we made up for no breakfast.

A hare here, bluebells there and the first may blossom in places; this felt like spring.
We had cycled 30 miles the day before the first hill that required us to walk, at Searby. Today, only 3 miles later, we were walking again. The scarp of The Lincolnshire Wolds must have been having an effect. We had been chatting lovingly as we went; it was one of those very sweet days together. The remote Rookery Farm gave us a secluded B&B with a delivery service from the nice Chinese people. Happy Days!

That was:
Bardney-South & West Kelsey-Searby-Barnetssby
35 miles

Mon Apr 24 From Barnetsby

Windy! At one point, I cycled at 12mph in order to progress at 3mph!
It all began with a cooler morning coming through the lower foothills of The Lincolnshire Wolds. The downs were glorious, the ups were vainglorious, or at least less glorious. At one early moment, I had a buzzard holding itself in the wind just above me, displaying every finger wing-feather. A primary education.

On the basis of 'use it or lose it," we patronise every remote café we find. Deepdale Cafe was no exception. Here, the more-stereotypical northern accent began. "'ave yer cooom far?" began the usual chat that spread to all the tables and we spent time with good folk with a wide variety of travel tales.

Our harshest spell of rain to date hit us at Barton-Upon-Humber but, just as we took shelter, it abated. We set off again but so did the rain. As a result, we were to be seeking new cycling gloves. When it came to the test, cheap ones proved exactly why they were 'cheap'.

Crossing Humber Bridge

At 155 metres (510 feet) high, The Humber Bridge was a colossus. I enjoyed the thrill of the views and the height. Cathy did not. Cathy had crossed a few high bridges in her time, particularly in New Zealand's mountain ranges, so I knew of her fear. I cycled behind her. She was the most stiff, motionless cyclist I have ever seen. It was 2 miles long! At the Hull end, she yelped with delight and a large portion of relief. I hugged her, knowing what feelings she had conquered to do it.

Through Hessle, the blossom petals had fallen on the wet ground and were picked up on our tyres. When I looked down onto my front tyre, I could see a rotating psychodelia of flower power. I felt all 60s-like! Barry of Bardney would have been proud of me!

Being the optimist and relative stupid, I suggested we could make a B&B nearly 20 miles further on. Bed and Breakfast places were few and far between on the banks of The Humber. We had spoken to Appletree Cottage last night but, considering the morning's weather, we had cancelled. It was cheeky, but we got reinstated on the basis that we could get there by 4.30pm. Then, we hit a fierce westerly wind from 12 miles out. No lunch, no water breaks, we just pedalled. Due to this, it was the most exhausting day so far. I was cycling along a perfectly fat road, up off the saddle, pushing my full body-weight into every rotation and I was only going 3 miles per hour. I could have walked faster! That was some wind.

When we got there (10 minutes to spare), we were greeted (an over-exaggeration to call it a greeting), not by the owner, but by a Baltic housemaid. Did she care?

She barely spoke, then was gone. "Sod her", we said, "Where's the bed?"

That was:
Barnetsby-Deepdale-Barton-Upon-Humber-Hessle-
N. Ferriby-Welton-Ellerker-Broomfleet-Faxfleets-
Blacktoft-Yokefleet-Laxton-Saltmarshe   35 miles

Tues Apr 25th (Day 15) From Saltmarshe near the Humber

Planning! It was all about planning. If we had got it wrong, all would have been lost. It would have been very easy to stay lost in the handsome parkland estate of the remote territory of Saltmarshe, but we weaved under yew arches, along lime-lined avenues and sped by suckling lambs. Then we hit wind. Was it worse than yesterday? Probably. Even downhill cycling was a push! All weather forecasters concurred: it was going to snow, so we had our smoked mackerel breakfast and left well before 8am in order to beat the snow due at 12. Rambling folk like us are not use to tight time restraints and this was the second day in a row! The oncoming snow also made us modify our intended route over The North York Moors. It now made eminent sense to listen to our cowardice and go round The Moors to the west over the next two or three days. Today, we aimed to be just short of York where we had phoned a B&B who would take us in early.

Villages hardly flashed by, but they went unnoticed. Crossing the M62 was more significant and passing the mighty power stations of Drax (UK's largest-ever producer of electricity) seemed to mean something in

56

our life. It also meant a move away from the River Humber north-westerly towards Selby, demonstrably into wind. This seemed more difficult for me, so Cathy was doing the encouraging as she noticed my ailing efforts behind her. She was clearly the stronger whereas I blamed my wider frame and heavier shoelaces.

I do love a confluence. We had already seen a fair few yet, at Barmby on the Marsh, the River Derwent flowed into the tidal River Ouse at such a picturesque location, and it brightened our gloomy day. The lock had Netherland ironmongery above it to reassure us of its solidity. It all needed to be substantial when those famous winter floods came off the Dales and Moors. From here, we clung to the Ouse by cycling on the path below the levee built as a flood defence. No tarmac, just a narrow, stony slither of a path for 2 miles, skirting Selby and heading towards Barlby, we cycled by an old mill works that caught the wind face on, bouncing it back onto us from its towering slab-side. Buffeted, Cath shouted back to me, "Careful," as busy traffic passed us. I wobbled, not able to direct the bike properly then, suddenly, the wind got right behind me and woosh, I was speeding. It was as if a big hand of Allah, or the lift from Our Lord had launched me downhill, yet I was on a flat road. Those were weird aerodynamics!

The ladies in Barlby's Café gave us free coffee and plenty of happy natter. That got us upwind for the final three miles, even if we were slowed by a runner wearing headphones who could not hear our bells and yells as we tried to pass.

The Dairyman's Cottage in Riccall, sympathising with our cause, had got our room ready by the time we arrived at 11.50am. We wrapped up warm then bussed the 10 miles into York for essential cycling bits only to be trapped in Waterstone's map section by a snowstorm. Downtown steaks and Brass Castle Ales were due compensation on our afternoon off.

That was:
Saltmarshe-Howden-Barmby-on-the-Marsh-Selby-Barlby-Riccall   17 miles

Wed 26 April From Riccall, 10 miles south of York

<u>Places ending BY</u>

How come all those places in Lincolnshire and Yorkshire end in "by"? I hear you cry. Ferriby, Barmby, Selby, Barlby and the like. Well, I found out. When the Vikings landed and raided a settlement, they gave it their surname and formally registered it with their law-masters, then it could be claimed to be owned by that leader "by law". This got shortened to just 'by'. Cute. Crumbly croissant breakfasts with Dot and the Leicester travel companions helped us decide our next move. We chose to set off and let the weather hit us. Five hours of rain was due to cover York from 10am to 3pm but the bright sky over the conservatory put some fire in our belly.

I guessed the 10 mile cycle route into York was once a railway line, but there was an oddity. Someone had created traditional white, wooden signposts at regular intervals, but the destinations were strange: "Saturn 746.000,000 miles" for example. All our planetary neighbours got a mention with mileage whereas "Earth" was simply "Here".

Cathy Riding The Knavesmire Mile

Our hedge-lined CR65 suddenly opened up to find York racecourse. Racing fans would be impressed to hear we rode the full mile of The Knavesmire Mile. Truly, we were on the cycle route that ran alongside the rails of the racing site that dates back to 1730. Elsewhere, but still in the York area, formal races had been recorded since 1530 and, in 1607 were even run on the frozen River Ouse. Climate change, eh? Well, The Romans had vineyards here in York. Must have been due to those diesel chariots.

Knavesmire was York's area for public hangings, yet it did not account for York-born Guy Fawkes. He was sentenced to death in London, of course, but he was never hanged. He fell off the gallows, broke his neck and the hangman was saved the bother.

We only saw enough of York's city centre to grab a coffee and get lost. Fortunately the river was always going to be downhill. When we got back to it, there was a Viking boat with oarsmen in convincing costumes being very unconvincing with the rowing. A high, steeped-stepped narrow river crossing then blocked our path to prove panniers and commuters do not tessellate. Mr Bean wrote the script.

No rain! How stupid or pessimistic are the Met Office boys and girls? Can they not read seaweed?

Our little nuggets of optimism urged us to phone ahead, believing the weather would hold for the afternoon. We heard of frost for the night, therefore we phoned B&B 14 miles ahead of us and we took it.

The River Ouse lost its urban look just beyond the last of York's northern warehouses and kept us company until Overton. Here, we came out of the lee of the trees and into the north –westerly wind. We even became thankful for the protection afforded by rural housing. This reminded me of a newspaper cutting from a flat area regarding the row of aspen trees planted by the local village's cricket team. It read, "you can feel the effect of them breaking wind for half a mile!"

At the National Trust's Benningborough Hall, we found a farm shop and a café. Such gems were few and far between, so never missed. Local cyclists took advantage, too so notes and natter were exchanged. Regional information was gathered and stored for the evening planning stages, often reshaping our intended passage.

The final 4 miles of the day to Linton-on-Ouse were undertaken on a full tank of 'Broccoli and Benningborough-Blue-Cheese soup' while our panniers were resplendently stocked with significant chunks of Farmhouse Quiche. We were not to starve over night.

That was:
Riccall-York Racecourse-York-River Ouse-Overton-Benningborough-Newton & Linton-on-the-Ouse   24 miles

Wed April 26 From Linton-Upon-Ouse, North Yorkshire

Fresh eggs, laid by the hens outside the door and cooked by the lady inside the house, set us on our way under light drizzle. The North York Moors were partially obscured by the rainfall. Their omnipresence had created a domineering panorama since yesterday afternoon, like the upturned hull of The Titanic across the northern horizon without eastern or western edges (yet). It must form a great practice ground and airspace for the midget jets on the airbase sitting on the edge of our overnight billet. Neat, sleek machines, they were; like Formula 1 cars on stilts and with wings. Such is the intensity of RAF training in the East of England, we have heard military aircraft on most days since Welney, Cambridgeshire. Either that or Putin has arrived unannounced.

As a consequence of changing our original route over The Moors via Hutton-le-Hole to avoid snow, we headed on the western detour into The Vale Of York. This did not mean we could ignore the great lump. The Kilburn White Horse soon emerged to tower above us as we sidled around to Thirsk by the back-lanes. There were hardly any off-road cycle paths this day yet the lanes were perfectly quiet enough. Intermittent drizzle restricted the numbers of walkers and cyclists in the wild, so our contact with fellow man was limited. Then we found the butchers at Helterby and the fine 'York Cycles Café' in Thirsk where we talked ourselves silly. It was also in Thirsk where we relinquished my binoculars; used maps and redundant clothing by posting them back home. All the packaging materials were kindly provided by the understanding café owner. We were shedding weight. Well, in the panniers at least.

Our bilateral enjoyment of the day was celebrated under the final rays of the sunny spell with our first ever raspberry magnum lolly. The tent was pitched just in time to enjoy listening to the heavy rain bouncing off our tent's 'canvas'.

That was:
Linton-Upon-Ouse-Helterby-Sessay-Sowerby-Thirsk-Kirby Wiske-Newby Wiske-South Otterington 32 Miles

Friday April 27 From South Ottertington

"Undulations" could have been today's title. We may have avoided The North York Moors, but we found some ripples from the hills this day. There was no point

63

mocking The Moors for not catching us either because the Pennines were waiting for us, visible all day to our west. Like Big Brother watching and waiting for us to come begging. They were still a few days away, but they commanded respect from the moment they appeared.

We had seen the trip's first stoat crossing the road yesterday and today's nature highlight was a pair of grey wagtails on The River Tees. Our first curlew since Kent appeared with the further delight of several yellowhammers. Lambs seemed to have been seen daily though rarely as numerous as today. Perhaps this was the first day where livestock exceeded arable farming. Our ability to digest and interpret our surroundings was due to the lack of rain or strong winds. Joy of joys.

We had left the Sustrans Cycle Routes that seemed a good idea until we got to a place called The Broad north of Newby Wiske. Here, we met plenty of traffic on, what appeared to be country lanes. Theories included a glut of cars due to the Tour de Yorkshire cycle race and the use of these lanes as a rat run between major roads. There were several occasions when our forward contract with Digenitas appeared superfluous.

Beyond Yannorth we found smaller lanes with fewer cars. Here, the local cycling clubs felt safe, too. Many sped by in either direction with a good deal of them taking the time to slow down for a chat or to give encouragement. One even yelled, "We saw you yesterday, how's it going?" Well, we were going fine, if a little tired from a night's camping next to a major railway line. Concentration, too, wore heavily on one's stamina, especially with so many potholes and blind summits.

Today's route through rural lanes meant we found nowhere for breakfast, so it was 12.30 before we got to the village shop in Appleton Wiske. We gobbled through a pie and a cake each like demons.

A newly gritted road then rattled our cages for 3 long miles and I was convinced that chippings stayed embedded in the range of orifices on offer. Then, by crossing the snaking River Tees with its flowering garlic roadsides, we were hailed into The Borough of Darlington without any sign of municipality.

We eventually found a town, though. A sort of outpost of council housing, imaginatively called Middleton St George. As a council-house boy myself, I am not fully qualified to sneer, but fully certified to make a judgement. Once we got a safe distance, at our B&B in Long Eaton, we came to the conclusion that Middleton St George was the official breeding ground for 'The Stars' of The Jeremy Kyle Show. Any lack of teeth appeared to be compensated by tattoos, beer bellies and shaved heads. And that was just the women.

We had picked The Vane Arms from a website earlier that day on the basis of it being the right distance to cycle and good reports on its food. Long Newton was a few miles out of Stockton-On-Tees, so we were hardly in Michelin Star country. The sight of the polite young landlady with metal stapled to her face also formed a prejudice. Therefore, the gorgeous evening meal was a revelation. We felt we had never had finer dining in any other pub. How about that! This was West End dining in County Durham.

That was:
South Ottertington-Warlaby-Yannorth-Danby Wiske-Deighton-Appleton Wiske-Hornby-Girsby-Low Dinsdale-Nearsham-Middleton St Geaorg-Long Newton   30 miles

---

EQUIPMENT (at this stage)
The bikes have stood up better to the shaking than me. I swore one day's bouncing was going to give me a stammer! Both front lights have been bounced off their frames with bungees holding them on. My lights do not work, so the weight of the redundant dynamo was despised. Cathy's rear-light's wiring had bounced out. The chains get loved and dry-lubed every other day. My gel-seat has got a hole in it. No punctures
The tent and all camping gear are all working well. Our new gizmo, a remote Internet EE Hub, had worked well when we needed it least but when we are out in the wilds, not sure of where we were and desperate for satellite assistance, there would be no signal whatsoever.

Saturday 29 April From Long Newton

Our cunning plan was hatched overnight: we would stay another night at The Vane Arms to attack the menu, leave the panniers at The Vane', cycle to Seaham or Sunderland, return to The Vane by train then get back to Sunderland tomorrow by train for the restart. Well it looked straightforward on the map!

Under grey skies, we cycled into Stockton, the home of the very first passenger train, to pick up the old railway line, now National Cycle Route 1, to Sunderland.

Simplicity ended in the maze of housing estates of Stockton.

When we did eventually find the trail, there were 9 awkward barriers to get through the urban mile. This local council must have been talking to the Kent aficionados.

The track coughed and spluttered until The Wynyard Centre, a Sustrans-inspired haven for cyclists to indulge in hot chocolate and sausage rolls. It was early, but we did not miss out. Whilst in the converted station, the local cycling club embraced us. News, views and clues were swapped, nearly a wife, too.

Now we were humming along. Newly leafed trees were either side; there were classic brick arched bridges to pass under and a well-financed surface to glide us northwards.

Somebody took a viaduct away. Just when we were not looking. Gone. The consequence stared at us from the top of an escarpment. We had obviously missed a turn to avoid this so, there we were, like lemmings on the edge….. a Butch Cassidy and Sundance Kid moment... Why we decided to tackle the steep hill down, I will never know, but forthright stupidity will be in there somewhere.

For the 200 feet descent, we walked our bikes down at such a steep angle they nearly flipped over our heads. Brakes were locked on yet gravity kept them sliding like a scree-run. It was gentle persuasion all the way: to our bikes, to ourselves and to each other. We made it without knowing how.

In the valley, curious round blocks, just two feet high, were the remains of the supporting pillars of a once mighty railway viaduct, destroyed in 1979 after 100 years of solidity.

We got into Thorpe Thewles and its valley with the old railway line continuing somewhere above us and to the north. "How do we get there?" we posed. Despite our fear of local knowledge, we were aided by a gent and were soon reunited with a glorious section through Hurworth Burns, the divided reservoirs. Gorse blooms threw heavy scent to intoxicate our senses. For a while there, I got the sudden urge to become a bee.

 A farmer had decided not to like the track any more, so the trail was diverted. We failed to notice this until we were forced back a mile. Whether or not it was the farmer that also turned the new route into a quagmire we were not certain, but he was our chief suspect. Farm gates were also built liberally along this detour to deter any pleasure from the experience. It appeared as no coincidence that we were running on the edge of Peterlee, so maybe the farmer had seen enough of his fellow humans. The sense of deprivation was not confined to the track surface. It did not help that the geography and industrial history had given them slag heaps. As a consequence, everything was black apart from the trees after the first foot of trunk. This was a shock after the earlier areas of magnesium limestone and its pastoral countryside. Once hitting the slag heaps, the black puddles hid their depth, some containing long-left articles of household waste with mangled kiddies' bikes being a regular feature. We picked our path through 5-year-old bin liners (once full, now spewing), long-emptied beer cans and the filth of modern life. Occasionally, we got off our bikes to ensure safe passage. 'Breakout' was onto bumpy gravel tracks where I reinstated a stammer.

The straightforward route on the map had not been so easy to follow on the ground. By South Hetton, we were following our nose more than the signs that were often vandalised by those with smaller minds than pockets or just brainless. We got lucky and found some smooth sections to The North Sea where we expected to hit Seaham yet never did. How did that happen?

One piece of cake had fortified us since our morning's sausage roll, so weariness accompanied us into Sunderland, the newly acclaimed "City". We asked a few people, "Where is the station?" before realising (from the range of the answers) there are many stations on Sunderland's Metro Line. We went too far for the main station, so we got the Metro back from the University Station, noticing a rear-wheel puncture as we did so. Yes, our first and it must have been the broken glass in the dark underpass. Cathy had avoided it all but I had no chance of avoiding it all in the gloom. Of course, this was the first day we left the panniers behind within which, oh dear oh dear, was the puncture outfit. I found a kit in Poundsavers but no pump. Cathy, on the other hand, found information and information was king. Or dark, as it turned out because it was Darke Cycles that she discovered. We both got new inner tubes and tyres while we chatted with the enthusiastic young anti-computer twenty-somethings. What a refreshing conversation. I hope, one day, they will rule the world.
Did we get the train back, as intended? No, there were all sorts of cancellations, so we went sly. Cathy had got the

sympathy of a taxi driver who did a deal on the basis he could chat her up all the way to Long Newton. Me? Well, I was tangled in the back sniffing the rubber of new tyres on two precariously placed bikes.

That was:
Long Newton-Stockton on Tees-Wynyard-Thorpe Thewles-Station Town-Shotton Colliery-South Hetton-Merton-Ryhope-Sunderland   39 miles

Sunday 30th April from Sunderland (restart from Long Eaton)

Our dear friend, Joan Nixon agreed to come to The Vane this evening, so we booked to stay again. We had to get back to Sunderland for the restart. This entailed a change at Thornby, a small provincial settlement, no more than a large village. Our wait for the Sunderland train was 35 minutes with the York train, in the other direction, due at 9.20am, 10 minutes before ours. Suddenly, while we sat in a foyer with 3 other people, cabs arrived. I would have believed anybody that told me that Paris Fashion Week had been moved to County Durham. 100 overtly over-dressed individuals, aged between 19 and 35, invaded the meagre space on offer. Wine bottles or cans of cocktails were embedded in most clenched fists. Some outfits appeared to be colour coordinated to Budweiser accessories! They said they were not going to a special event, just having a boozy day out in York. The Bank Holiday session seemed to be a tradition in the area. Judging by the height of the stilettos, trips to A&E were on the cards, too. A mixture of aroma filled the air as the perfume clouds coalesced around us. Then they were gone, herded into the standing-room only coaches already packed with like-minded wannabes. Once they left, we helped to pick up at least one smashed bottle and several crushed cans.

Cramming them in!!

Any thought that York was the lone target went when our train to Sunderland arrived. The clientele may have been more rounded, but that automatic instinct to open a fancy can prevail. Vodka & lime, rum & coke, gin & tonic, even frozen cocktails; pssst! Pssst! Pssst!! sip-chat, sip-chat, sip-chat!

Like all cities, Sunderland confused us. Monumental icons always help, as the Wearmouth Bridge did here. Built in big-boy Meccano-set style, it yelled 'solidity' and a safe cycle lane headed to the sea. Once on the coastal cycle path, however, things got dangerous. The on-shore crosswind was strong enough to slew us across he path and towards the oncoming traffic, so we walked. Cathy was shaken by this as well as the noisy traffic that, away from town speed restrictions, sped by. Respite came from a few coastal buildings and then a wide track that is used for The Great North Run, a race in which Cathy once competed.

Marsden Rock came into view somewhere in South Shields, a huge lump to me on my first view but a diminished one to Cathy as it had been battered by the sea for over 40 years since her first sighting. The wind was still strong but the sun was out, so the view across the rock and beyond to the headland of The Tyne estuary was mighty. Here, we turned away from the wheeling sea birds and inland through South Shields.

A local said she had lived in the area all her life yet had never been on The Tynemouth Foot Ferry. Well, we did with several other cyclists and an elderly couple thrilled to hear of our adventure. From them, we heard tales of the shipbuilding era where he had spent his whole life in the steel foundry without ever owning a car.

From the pier on the north bank, it was 10 miles to Newcastle Station, a route blessed with the husbandry of a caring council. On the way, we cycled under the arch declaring the start of the Hadrian's Wall Cycle Route, focusing our mind on what we were about to attempt. I nursed my bike into The Hub, a cycle workshop in Newcastle on the riverbank. Here, Mariusz made two bolts from an aluminium rod to refit my bike-stand, then recommended a service tomorrow. We booked it for both bikes.

From The Hub, the Millennium and Tyne bridges were visible all the way through a vintage bus fair; a live rock group gig and around 20 market stalls to the gloriously grand station. A train back? Simple, surely. "Have you got bike reservations?" the attendant asked.

"What?" was the only answer available to us. Apparently, the Virgin trains only take a maximum of 5 bikes, sometimes only 3, so one needs a reservation ticket.

The size of Newcastle station was daunting, especially from platform 11 with 4 minutes before our train was due. I caught Cathy's bike as she fled over the stairs to rescue the situation if, indeed, it could be rescued with reservations available. Cathy, of course, saved the day.

Haway the lads! We had cycled to Newcastle!

Our evening, indeed our whole journey in the North East, was made complete by the lovely Joan Nixon. Our family friend and fellow fell walker became a widow last year when her fun husband Jim died. Love poured like the tales. What a gorgeous person, dear friend and great company,

That was:
Sunderland-Marsden Rock-South & North Shields
viaTynemouth Ferry-Eldon-Newcastle 25 miles
(plus 6 miles to/from stations)

At 3am, the pub owner broke into his own pub. We guessed he had been on a bender. In the morning, an almost full packet of cigarettes and a very full wallet were on the ground in a secured compound outside the broken kitchen window. We left without seeing anybody.

Monday May 1 From Newcastle (after restart from Long Newton)

Theories of the break-in were discussed but we agreed to leave them to their family bliss. Our best contribution would be a high mark on Trip Advisor. We cycled 3 miles to the local station and landed back at The Hub in Newcastle for the services to our over-'lubed' bikes. Yeah, my fault, I thought lots of oil was good for them. During the two and half hour wait, we chomped through bacon sandwiches to service our stomachs. Mind you, we were made to jump involuntarily when Cathy's rear inner tube exploded. Darke Cycles of Sunderland had pinched the tube so, when Mario heaped up the pressure, BOOM!!

New bolts, gear cables, chain guards and brake cables all got fitted, plus a new spoke or two that I had managed to snap somewhere. If only there was a Hub for old people!

Up the Tyne valley we went, assuming the local vibes about it being a flat-ride to Hexham were true. Wrong.

Pretty, scenic and mostly car-free: it was but the last 8 miles were full of hills. The nadir point was 1½ mile in when it all went "technical". A plastic wire-protector under my rear mudguard had got flipped by a stick or stone or passing green Martian. Thirty greasy minutes ensued.

In one respect, we were elated because the kind club cyclists who stopped to help could not find the fault, so we felt rather good to have dealt with it ourselves. Mariusz had said we should now think of ourselves as cyclists. It was beginning to sink in that we were starting to qualify.

There was still time for more dramatic problems if we didn't keep smart. The May Bank Holiday crowds were out, packing the many car parks on the way. A survey once discovered that 80% of tourists never stray more than 400 yards from their car and this was borne out, but around those areas we had to dodge ice-cream queues, two-year olds on scooters and dogs on extending leads. Without Cathy's warnings, I would have wiped out a nursery class and racked up some large vet bills.

Thoughts of splattered spaniels and pummelled poodles remained on our minds as the Tyne became shallower, with areas of natural waterfalls as we glided into the centre of ancient Hexham.

That was: Newcastle-Blaydon-Prudoe-Corbridge-Bank Foot-Hexham Hexham 25 miles (+3 to the station)

Tues May 2nd From Hexham

Over The Pennines! Well, it will take two days but we hoped this would be part one of two. These Pennines lasted a long time, but we had yet another cunning plan: leave all but one pannier (the one with the puncture repair kit) in the hotel, cycle to Haltwhistle light as a feather, then get the train back this evening. Tomorrow's train would take us to restart at Haltwhistle. Understood? Us neither.

The CR72 (Hadrian's Wall Way) had a passion for views over the River Tyne Valley. Early doors, we were close enough to see 40 yards of riverbank festooned with a magical carpet of cowslips, near Fourstones. Then we were up, scorching thigh muscles like burgers on a barbeque. I could hear mine sizzle.

This was our longest climb yet, confirmed by every conceivable sinew in my legs. The high points were formed by desolate moorland that chilled us quickly. I have been prone to phone my Mum from these obscure, remote spots, which can be fun but this had an edge. "Hello, Ma, sorry, must go."

Once up on the high shoulders it was not constant as one would imagine; it was up and down and up again, and, well you guessed it. A left hand turn engaged The Tyne Valley love affair once again, but it was 2½ miles of sharp downhill, freewheeling with yelps. 3 miles of up and down led us to Bardon Mills Stores which doubles as an oasis and a tearoom of heavenly portions. Yes, the cakes were large. Exaggerations, only maybe, but in the absence of any other cafe all day, we elevated this establishment to a pinnacle. It was while we were in the cosy retreat that we realised we were ahead of time. We were set on getting the 3 o'clock train back from Haltwhistle but, by mentioning the 1 o'clock train, we were setting ourselves a stiff time constraint. The last 5 miles had to be done in just over 20 minutes. Given the hills and our heavy bikes, we were always going to be pushing it. We flew along, up and down the ensuing river terraces, but the views were still stunning. Pumped-up thigh muscles could propel us faster and faster on the flat areas, so those miles felt marvellous for two over-60 year olds. And, yes, we made the train.

A little note on local Northern trains: they have a policy of supporting sustainable transport (not just talk about it on posters), so each train has an area containing rubber sleeves that accept the front wheel of a bike. Simple, but effective. There are parts of the Rail Network that should listen to Northern folk.

That was:
Hexham-Fourstones-The Pennines Part 1- Nr Haydon Bridge-Bardon Mill-Haltwhistle 20 miles

Wed May 3rd From Haltwhistle

Someone had calculated the centre spot of mainland Britain and come up with Haltwhistle. This gave us the belief that we were half way there without any constructive argument or mental strength to counter claim. Had we realised the day would end *south* rather than north of Haltwhistle, we could have argued that half way was still to come. Beyond these hypotheses, we knew we were heading west and thankful of a northeasterly wind to aid our uphill climbs. In truth, we walked 8 or 9 hills and most of those were once we were on "the way down." I will explain, soon.

We reached the watershed of The Pennines inside 2 hours. It was a joyful moment when we had cycled to the hilltop, then looked around to find that all the other, plentiful hills was below us. This occurred in a nameless place beyond Gilsland and we felt mighty.

Very soon we were inspecting the Roman Fort remains at Birdoswald.

Hadrian's Wall near the top of The Pennines

An American couple from Boston spoke to me as I followed Cathy up the hill after we parked our bikes. I asked if they were enjoying the UK and explained our journey before they pushed onto the fort. Cathy, herself was chatting with a fellow cross-Pennine cyclist from

Garstrang who had previously cycled from The Isle of Wight to Stornaway. He took a photo of us and our sign which immediately appeared on The Garstrang Cycling Club website. Wow! We became deep in note-swapping conversation when the returning Boston man came and rudely stood between Cathy and "Mr Garstrang", ignoring the on-going discussion. Staring close to Cathy, he asked, "Which one of you guys is the psychiatrist?"
"Neither," replied Cathy.
"Hell, on that bike journey, one of you should be," he smarmed, but he soon cowered away with Cathy's immediate put-down, "On a day like today, it is people who are NOT on such a bike journey who need a psychiatrist!"

The next (giggling) mile was our fastest yet: a healthy decline resulting in breakneck speed on a well surfaced road. We flew. It was, however, not as straight forward as that for the full descent from the Pennine Peak. Cumbria's side of our nation's backbone had water-cut valleys that scarred our way. Some very sharp-angled downward stretches were followed by equally severe walk-climbs with a loaded bicycle to push. Coffee and cake indulgences took place at Lanercost Priory where the vicar joined others in swapping Hebridean tales.

This was a very fine day of powder blue sky and endless sunshine. From our lofty ledge we could see the peaks of The Lake District and those of the Scottish Uplands. Exciting times. Before the day ended, there was a final landmark moment: the crossing of the path of our Land's End to John O'Groats Walk. This occurred when we walked the other way across the Victorian bridge over The Eden in Wetheral. Soon after, Alan Jackson pick us up to enjoy the warm Cumbrian hospitality of Alan and his wife, Pat, a life-long friend of Cathy's. Theirs is a richly grained friendship all round.

That was:
Haltwhistle-Greenhead-Willowford Walk Turrets-Birdoswald-(All along The Watchtower that was Hadrian's Wall)-Lees Hill Turrets etc-Lannercost Priory-Brampton-Hayton-Gt Corby-Wetheral
28 miles

Thurs May 4th From Wetheral

Alan's father, who lived in the homely Cumbrian settlement of Wetheral, had kept our bikes and camping gear in his garage overnight. Oh, yes, our arrangements were often complicated but they all had worked (so far). Another cunning plan had been hatched whereby the Jacksons retained all but one of our panniers. They would carry them to our next B&B in Annan, Scotland (booked that morning), so we could dine together again. Understood?

So we got to cycle over Wetheral's magnificent viaduct again to get back in touch with CR72 towards Carlisle.

A road sign declared "Carlisle 4" miles but the cycle routes liked to keep one safe and in so doing doubled the distance. We stayed safe.

80

The River Eden, Near Wetheral: Our LEJO crossing point.

Rickerby Park, on the outskirts of Carlisle, sat resplendent on this sunny day at 15°C in a brisk north-easterly. For the most part, this was a helpful tailwind but we were buffeted from the side (spring rolls, prawn vol-au-vents, cocktail sausages). This hampered us (pork pie, coleslaw, bunch of grapes and quiche).

Short cuts during the day saved us 10 miles, though each was taken with an element of guesswork. Our route through Rickerby Park was the first. This got us onto CR7, which I thought we had seen in Lincolnshire but they were all becoming a blur in the memory.

In Rockcliffe, on the English side of the Scottish border, there was The Crown & Thistle, so named in celebration of James VI of Scotland taking to the English throne as James I. We did not know that reasoning of the pub name. We were learning lots! A gentile set of, let us say, over-ripe folk were having a coffee morning there, some 25 or more of them. One spotted our "Dover to Cape

Wrath" sign, so I obliged in giving a 20-minute talk that tumbled into a two-way banter on our adventures before we were allowed coffee.

Three miles on, we slid onto "The All Purpose Road". It is not signed as such but all locals know it by that name. It ran up the side of the M6 across the border into Scotland and inevitably Gretna. Look down on it when you next pass that way. The close proximity of a motorway while cycling meant we were in a wall of sound. We had no idea if the noisy thunder of a lorry was coming from our road or the motorway. As well as the deafening hubbub, the strong side-wind made us unsure that we were going to remain upright. Such fears drove us to dismount and walk the last mile and a quarter to the edge of Gretna. This famous border settlement, with its blacksmith's registry office looked quaint apart from the frantic through-traffic.

Once on the back-road, we found the old artillery road with its ex-railway line used for "the Devil's Porridge", a dangerously poisonous ordnance chemical made innocently by women workers during the 1st and 2nd World Wars. None made old age. The fireless Sir James train used for the chemical transport was on display at Eastrigg museum. The "Sir James" was pumped with steam at 4 stations on a 40 miles stretch of production line, so the ammunitions saw no spark or fire.

The scenery and generally flat cycling made it a good day if we forget the scary bits. We had crossed the estuarine Eden and Esk rivers then made the meaningful passage into Scotland. Yes, "Dover to Scotland" sounded rather good. The forward southern view was dominated by The Solway Firth, a low tract of silt deposits and naturally graded stones-cum-rocks. To our southeast were the high ridges of The Lake District, in a haze of sunshine and a dewy veil.

Entering Scotland

It all passed too quickly. This was not entirely down to our speed but the ever-changing vistas in these grand places. Fast roads and the chance of an afternoon rest drove us on, so the busy town of Annan was soon engulfing us. The four-poster bed in our reasonably priced B&B was grand.

The diligent Jacksons arrived with the panniers and whisked us off to Lockerbie's Ravensfield Hotel and the dottiest hotel proprietors known to man. Good food, good friends but the owners needed an audience. Sadly (and tellingly) we were the only ones they had all night.

PUBLICANS:
If you really value customers, recognise what they are there for. The Lone Booze-head is easy. The Two Lovers are, too. The Boaster will enjoy your chat and tell you how he has done it better. You will rarely get the Nosey Natterer, the type that is just as interested in your bathroom grouting as you are. However, if you ever spot The Two Couples Who Are Life Long Friends (and maybe they have even told you that is what they are) leave them alone. They will not care about batteries to your remote phones or how the local doctor likes his fish cooked. On these occasions, Landlord, learn to shut up.

That was:
Wetheral-Lt Corby-Warwick Bridge-Crosby-Carlisle-Rickerby Park-Rockcliffe-Gretna-Eastrigg-Annan 28 miles

Fri May 5th From Annan, Scotland

Our lovely B&B ladies busied themselves while the man of the house busied himself as a very fat plonker whose fingers had never been lifted.

In the world outside, Annan gave us a Scottish salmon River, The Nith, to ride alongside until we, and it, met The Solway Firth. There was no need for coffee at the caravan site on the edge of the estuary, but the scenery dictated it.

High headlands and distant mountains dominated the land, white bluebells (whitebells?) and gorse hedges trimmed into rectangles, adorned it. Back lanes and converted railway lines gave us safe passage into Dumfries. Here, we got 2 soups, 2 pies and 2 cream cakes for £6.28, surely half the price of the southern equivalent. On the edge of town, an angler was 'worming' for salmon and sea trout and, in-town, the salmon leaps tumbled without its migrants near Rabbie Burns 's House. As with most conurbations, the cycle route signs either disappeared or they were placed every 200 yards when they are not needed. Once clear of the suburbs, we were on country lanes that roller-coastered over miles with the occasional water-cut valley to annoy our muscles but delight our senses.

By afternoon, the Friday-Get-Away Traffic sped past at frightening rates. Even their roof-boxes looked scared. This was a day when we pushed on, gained a decent Suntan and, in the most part, benefitted from a northwesterly wind. At 40 miles, this was our longest yet (a tad more than yesterday), yet we had achieved it fully laden, so we deserved a quiet night on the campsite. We wondered if that would be possible on a Friday night. We also deserved ale.

Off we went to become the only customers (on a Friday night!) in a seedy Indian restaurant, looking at contours on our OS maps. "Can we really do this?"... "How much food can we carry?".... "Are you sure?" Under our wonderful taunt tent that held true in the wind, we slept soundly, wondering...

That was: Annan-Powfoot-Ruthwell (Savings Bank Museum!!)-Bankend-River Nith-Dumfries-Lochfoot-Milton-Haugh of Orr-Castle Douglas 40 miles

Sat May 6th From Castle Douglas

Happy Birthday, Son.
Phil and the cycling mechanics at Studio Velo Bike Shop
did us proud with a complete brake-pad change and
check over. The theory of 60psi on the front tyres and 85
on the rear sounded good at the time but this bulked the
tyres up to such an extent that we had zero tolerance on
the rear mudguards. As a result, somewhere along the
road, Cathy's bike developed a Quack with every
rotation and mine sounded like a violent red grouse.
Returning and re-joining the queue for the bike repair
shop gave us waiting time to sample Scotland's café
culture. It appeared to be stuck in the 1960s where the
flapjacks were wafer thin in terms of seeded material yet
covered with a layer of icing three times as thick and
sturdy. Little wonder that a 2016 study found two thirds
of Scots are overweight or obese.

Our belated departure at 12.30 did not faze us but the
belief (several times) that we had lost something *did*
perturb us. Due to my regained fitness, the weight of the
panniers was now evenly distributed between us. Such
changes meant we no longer knew where things were.
Order had been lost! Frantic searches always found that
which we felt lost, but not until a roadside kerb had seen
most of our worldly possessions scattered liberally over
a yard or two. By the fourth time, it got a bit fractious
because we knew what was missing: our memory.

It did not help that we were both wondering about the
big hills that we were yet to find. Everyone we spoke
with could not offer a way round them, so we began to
doubt ourselves in the strong northerly winds around at
the time. We even talked about how gallant we should

feel in failure, knowing we had tried our hardest therefore we could take honour in defeat.

In the meantime, we had some fun going south to a peninsular where the boldly named Kirkcudbright nestled in an estuary. God knows I tried to pronounce it properly but never did. Our route (The Seven, but it was not a bore) skimmed the high-water-line to the sea. Diamonds danced on the sea as the sun reflected on the chop. It was a stunning point on another day's beautiful passage. Our course then took us inland then back to the sea again in more of a southwesterly direction than of late. There was Kirk Andrew whose castle still looked capable of inhabitancy. Inland again, we found the healthy community of Borgue. A few miles later, I declared I was "Beyond Borgue". I always fancied myself as a great tennis player.

The last 8 miles were north facing, so they were awful. Respite eventually came in the Galloway Forest and through the magnificently maintained Hilly Hotel Golf Club, where unseen red squirrels were in residence. This remoteness took us to the heart of The Gatehouse of Fleet, the poshest place in the county of Dumfries and Galloway. It was 5pm, our day had been full and began late, so 25 miles was as good as 35 on another day. We found The Murray Arms to our lilking, which was a good job as it was the only lodgings for miles. Home for the night.

Before I sleep, I need to mention the native bluebells in such unspoilt native land. We met the native humans and, those we understood, were happy folk; as rich in conversation as their surroundings.

Another magical moment of colourful splendour occurred today. A local in a car tooted as he passed on our right. On our left, a flock of oystercatchers took flight like a pack of cards being thrown to the air, piping their call of alarm. The old heron had heard all this before. Like a dedicated angler, he was aware of the furore yet unmoved. There were more fish to be caught.

That was:
Castle Douglas-Kirkcudbright-Kirk Andrew-Borgue-Gatehouse of Fleet 19 miles

Sun May 7th From Gatehouse of Fleet

Kippers and DIY bicycle maintenance began the day. Our determination to kill a duck and a grouse from our rear mudguards proved worthless, so we set off quacking and churring. No cloud crossed our sky but a mature roe deer crossed our path just 10 yards away. The climb through coppiced woodland kept us in sublime dappled light, although our thighs were not quite as delighted. A calling cuckoo was in the glen above us as we ascended, so we had the delight of rising above this charming caller as it remained on its favoured tree while we reached the top. No one else turned up or down. For an hour and a half we never saw a soul..... then Cathy went to have a pee... guess what!

Craggy fells and rounded hills were on our same level for a while but we were always destined to return to sea level. Creetown was on The Cree estuary and, from one point on the hills, it was a 5-mile downhill glide. No pedalling, but many manoeuvres around potholes.

There was nowhere open for coffee, so a now-local London lass warmly assured us, so we pressed on into open country with further assurances of our own that there was nowhere for coffee. Solace was found in the form of the crumbled remains of Wednesday's crisps on the top of a 1-in3 hill that commandingly overlooked a broad bend in The Cree River.

It was a day in the Borders with its ups and downs, open and shut gates, walked hills and cutting sunrays. These factors helped us form the excuses to stop early today, at Newton Stewart (brother Rod was not in town, probably sailing).

Shall I bore you with B&B the story? Despite the sunny day, a frost was forecast. We needed a good night's sleep to prepare for going "over the top" tomorrow. Okay. We booked a B&B less than 24 hours ago, then cancelled it because we felt we were going further. Realising we were not going further, we rebooked it through Booking.com. We sat outside the B&B from 2.15 to 5.45 before Booking.com confirmed they had sent an email booking but had not heard from the owners. The owners called to say that, as we had cancelled, they went to Glasgow for the day. Another B&B, 50 yards away would take us in as long as we did not queer the local entente cordiale. Eventually, 4 hours after we hit town, our Cubes (the bikes) were safe in a shed for the night while we, emotionally drained found a cheap Italian meal and zeds in minutes.

That was:
Gatehouse of Fleet-Creetown-Newton Stewart
24 miles

Mon 8th May From Newton Stewart

Cathy was not entirely well but willing to see how we got on. There was a strong chance that we would end up in the great voids of nowhere we were about to launch ourselves into. To accommodate this possibility, we heaped grain bars from The Mid-Scotland Co-Op into our panniers.

Glentrool Visitor Centre was 9 miles away, close to the source of The Cree River, so that was to be our first judgement point. Glen Trool, in 1307 saw martyrs slaughtered for their beliefs and we believed we could cycle over these hills? We might slaughter ourselves.

Information came in flurries over fruit scones; a borrowed ordnance survey map and two keen cyclists convinced Cathy that we could make it. Local knowledge gave us the confidence in the plan to leave CR7 in preference of a devious route we had never previously considered (well, I had not). Fears had reigned for many days regarding the height we were going to climb using heavy touring bikes. The newly proposed route would take us higher but avoided an extra down-and-steep-up called The Devil's Elbow and The Nick of Balloch (sounds like a vasectomy). We fell for it and went for it.

Going Over The Southern Uplands Galloway Ridge
Phil of Studio Velo, Castle Douglas can claim an understatement: he said, "Oh, yeah, it's a bit exposed." Desolate, bleak, barren and uninhabitable only starts to describe the place. There we were: two rather old people on bikes that cronked back to the ravens on each wheel rotation, full-on into a north easterly, racked up to the nines with camping gear we had barely used, crossing 20 miles between the last settlement and the next one. This

scenario could hardly be captured by the words "a bit exposed".

More regular folks will know of Hardknott Pass in The Lake District. Well, today, we climbed over 100 feet more. And, from sea level! Mind you, this smugness only arrived after the event. We could look back in pride, but at the time it pushed us very hard. On some occasions, we walked for a quarter of a mile or so, not always on the uphill sections, just to hear and sense the silence. That was until the occasional log lorry (pulling not one but two bogies) hammered by within inches of our brake blocks.

Cathy and Log Lorry (doing 60mph) at very close quarters

Just how cold it was on the flat, 2 miles of 'top' was not realised until we stopped climbing on our pedals to make them turn. Then came the descent: steep and long.

Once on it, we thrived on the freedom until our sweat dried (or froze?), then we felt the chill of the air as we sped at 30mph for 8 miles, probably the longest downhill run we found. Cathy yelled that she needed to stop and I saw how pale she had become, shivering too. Not quite hypothermic, but not far short. I threw clothes over her and sat her in the sun.

Recovery led to elation. Achievement led to appreciation. With mossy fells as our backdrop, we cuddled.

The next 8 miles were all about treating ourselves to a luxury B&B. John's "Gardenrose" in Maybole was it, an Arts & Craft house designed by Charles Rennie Mackintosh. The other guest, Ian Knox was born locally (of Ayrian race?) and joined us for dinner at the nearest pub, 5 mikes away. The B&B landlord was our free taxi! Ian, 75 was back in the area to follow the last, unfinished work of Robert Louis Stevenson. The book was titled "A Walk Through Carrick" (the old name for the area involving the counties of Ayrshire and Galloway) which happened to cover Ian's genealogical past. A fun time.

I will leave the day with a neat quote from Stevenson:
"I travel not to go anywhere, but to go. I travel for travel's sake. The great affair is to move."

That was: Newton Stewart-Glentrool-Kirk Michael-Maybole   38 miles

Tues May 9th   From Maybole, Ayrshire

Will we make the ferry to Arran today?
Bright, not too breezy yet there was a nip in the air to surprise us. I guess that summed up the weather as we

bumbled over the awful surface of the B1024 out of Maybole. It was like riding over a rubble strip of fixed piano keys.

Rabbie Burns was born in the next town, Alloway. An industry surrounds the humble shack that saw him enter this world and a tearoom was advertised, our real target. Culturally astute, we maybe but we were on a mission. Sadly, the tearoom was shut.

Elsewhere, the Scented Garden tearooms overlooked the lip-smacking River Doon. I stared deep into the peaty currents, transfixed as I spoke to my darling wife, promising to bring her back for a romantic trip with a chance of a wild salmon. However, Cathy had gone inside so, as I turned away from the watery glides, I saw the lady I was engaging was alone, startled and slightly flattered.

We veered left away from the busy B road. Its almost constant threat from fast cars got to Cathy, so re-joining CR7 on the promenade was a delight, apart from the shockingly cold sea breeze on our uncovered legs. The morning sunshine had convinced us that shorts were a good idea. The shorts weren't even a tasteful fashion statement. Fully trousered-up, we imagined the last 25 miles to the ferry as a doddle; a flat surface all the way.

Doctors must have prescribed a walk for the wobbly masses of Ayr. Large men and women in their 40s with walking sticks and bellies like beach balls, sagging knee-bound, toiled on the promenade. It was agony watching their grimacing faces. Seeing us in glimmering lycra was not helping. Scottish poor diet is legendary and here was its manifestation. We hoped their hard-earned yardage in glorious fresh air gave them the impetus they needed for a change in lifestyle. Fair play to the Ayr doctors or whoever had launched this craze.

The gliding promenade lasted less than two miles before we were diverted to back streets, industrial estates and railway crossings. This deteriorated into a very poor route. Hope sprung occasionally, if not eternally, alongside the many golf courses. Turnberry had been to our south before we joined the links coast, but from Ayr a series of links courses followed with Royal Troon embedded within them. A golfer declared there were 20 golf courses within walking distance of one another. Prestwick golf course, the home of the first ever Open (1860) offered both fairway and runway. Flights of both A380s and birdies can be seen there.

Gorse in full bloom dominated the courses' boundaries, with tonal greens and happy heather forming the framing background. Those sections were sweet, but there were too many intersections with roads. When tired, these can bring the sense of an accident into the mind. This played heavily on Cathy's mind as she had to take the lead with a partially sighted idiot behind, depending on her. Rightly or wrongly, she believed my problem was hers. I was not sure if my bubbly enthusiasm just made things worse for her but, later, we both realised it was our differing attitudes that got us through the sticky bits.

Signposts were often used for solace yet, when we read TROON 5; then cycled a mile Troon-bound, then saw TROON 6, we could have become disheartened. Worse still was the town we will always know as Irving 5. No matter where we went for nearly an hour, it appeared as if it was the first half of a football result.

Back to back days of 40 miles had taken their toll by the Ardrossan ferry terminal, so any elation had a flat-tyre element to it. Then, by the time we sailed into The Isle of Arran (a one-and-a-half hour crossing that included engine failure), our elation had benefitted from a metaphoric puncture repair. So we celebrated.

Goat Fell, Isle of Arran
(I know not to where it fell)

A bay walk under Goat Fell (2,867ft) gave us time alongside nesting ringed plovers and a mountain stream where a red-breasted merganser fed at close quarters in clear water. Then we found The Fiddlers bistro bar with its Folk Music in full swing. With no champagne on offer, we raised glasses of prosecco on our achievement of reaching a Scottish Island by bicycle! We tried to remember each overnight stop we had taken from Dover but the music and Arran whisky just would not let us. It was the first time I had heard Leonard Cohen's Hallelujah sung in Gaelic and it was magical.

If I am looking for and adjective for that evening, I think the word would be gleeful.

That was:
Maybole-Alloway-Ayr-Prestwick-Troon-Irving-Saltcote-Ardrossan-Brodick, Arran 40 miles

Wed May 10th From Brodick, Isle of Arran

This was always destined to be a short day's cycle as we needed to get from one side of Arran to the other. The port on the northern side would allow us to catch the ferry to The Mull of Kintyre tomorrow. Does Paul McCartney still live there?
Question: what has Paul McCartney, Gordon Brown and Harold Wilson got in common? They were all christened with the same first name as me, James, yet never used it!

The start of today's simple journey got postponed. Administration surrounding medication bored us until 2.45pm in Brodick. Two hours later, we had skimmed the east coast, climbed up, into, through and back down from the heart of the enchanted isle.

The only place on the way was Corrie. My lovely daughter, Laura would love to appear in Corrie, but not that one. This was the last village on the east coast on a ledge below the hills, probably a raised beach. The only way was up, pushing for most of it. We found four different cuckoos calling which gave us a nearly-continuous contact with their kind, a rare opportunity back home in the Home Counties these days.

The central two miles saw a down hill section then what *seemed* like a further down hill section. It happened to be an optical illusion. At one point I stopped to check that both wheels spun without mudguard friction or faulty brake. It was very weird. Later, we checked the OS map to find it was definitely uphill, but our eyes will always insist it went down!

The central area was a bowl with a water-eroded area at it deepest point, so we had a steep climb to get back out of it. From its upper rim, there were 3 miles of freewheeling with the brake blocks taking a bashing but the bay below was beautiful. Who said Bs were scarce?

Descending from the fells, we found Lochranza, a very small seaport. We settled into our B&B and chatted about the offshore views of cycling around and through an island, an unusual experience for us. The scenery on either coastal side gave us panoramas of lengthy tracts of mainland Britain a few miles over the sea off Arran. On the Brodick side, we had been running parallel with Ayrshire as it slipped into Glasgow, whereas Lochranza faced the extraordinarily long lump of The Mull of Kintyre.

Arran's Lochranza with Mull of Kintyre ahead

As I write this at 9.30pm (and after our first hint of evening midges), three mature red deer (hinds) are feeding about 15 yards from our bed. They have been on the hill for an hour at eye level to our pillows. Good night, deer.

That was:
Brodick-Corrie-Lochranza   15 miles

Thurs May 11th From Lochranza by ferry

Our early morning entertainment was a red squirrel on the lawn: such a fluffy fellow. This was always going to be our lowest mileage day in terms of cycling, yet still momentous in terms of travel.

Ferry termini do not come any sweeter than the one we enjoyed under the dispersing, wispy clouds at Lochranza. Settled seas of stainless steel soothed our way to the Mull of Kintyre, 5 miles by ferry. This leg of land sweeps south-westward from the mainland, similar to the Stranraer peninsular. Both seem geographically awkward and are odds-on favourites for severance from the mainland in a millennium or two, given some lusty storms. Our only major physical task was to cycle from one side of 'Kintyre to the other, yet even this was a tough up-and-down effort. We were getting used to Scotland's preference for "non-flat". The lack of habitation made it look like good eagle country, despite not seeing any good eagles, or bad ones. What we encountered were local 4x4 vehicles dashing across the isthmus, attracted to the ferries like army ants to their food source. Throughout all this, one cuckoo or another called. It was during this crossing that we met Mark, a fellow cyclists who admitted to struggling just as much as we were, yet he was 40 years our junior. How pleased were we to hear that?

Gliding wheels eased us down to the second ferry of the day, on the far side of 'Kintyre, that would take us 30 miles to the island of Islay. The freshly laid tarmac was a true delight as we looked down to the narrow inlet that contained our ferry terminal, Kennacraig. We arrived with an hour and a half to spare. The first hour went well, then horror struck: we found a bore. I guessed the poor wife had endured her husband's pessimism for long enough to earn canonisation. She had probably suffered sufficient agony to get away with murder on the grounds of psychological abuse.

They arrived on a tandem, the vehicle they had taken here, there and everywhere, he declared. We got the list. After 20 minutes of his "we have done it all", we explained, almost timidly, that we were not cyclists really but had arrived there having cycled from Dover. He immediately slammed us with, "Journeys do not interest _us,_ they don't hold _value_. No, when _we_ get somewhere, we _really_ enjoy a circuit." Off he went again on how great he was (his wife visibly cringed).

His mistake was to tell us he was about to be on the same ferry and staying in the same hotel as us. This gave us time to develop tactics for avoidance, which served us well over the next two days. The closest we got to getting caught was in the hotel garden, but Cathy's dance-of-the-tea-trays shook them off at every turn. Anyway, back on The Mull of Kintyre...
Kennacraig was tucked deep in the gullet of an eight-mile sea loch where navigation restricted the speed of the ferry, so the engines went up a notch at the mouth with open sea ahead.

It was a two-hour sail to Port Askaig on Islay, where the sea currents in the strait with Jura were turbulent even when seemingly flat. I think sailors call this "busy water" where it seems to boil internally without wave or swell. It was the finest example I had ever seen since the tide-race at the old chain crossing from Glenelg to Skye. These were scary waters.

I felt sorry for Islay because all the cameras clicked at Jura's daunting peaks.
There was something heavenly about the thought of not cycling for two days. Sun-filled, still air made us almost skip up into Islay's coastal woodland of predominantly

silver birch. We found a small, three-acre loch dwindling in drought conditions yet apparently healthy. A colony of competing, rare wood white butterflies played like confetti in dappled rays. Even in my days as a British Butterfly Conservation Society counter, I had never seen the likes of this.

Over dinner, we counted that Islay was the 57th island that we had set foot on together. It is a romantic game to play because it brings back the diverse memories. Haggis, neeps and samples of Islay's famed waters prepared our way, or sway, to easy sleep.

That was: Lochranza on Arran-ferry to Claonaig on Mull of Kintyre-Kennacraig- ferry to Port Askaig on Islay 7 miles of cycling

REST DAYS AND TRAVEL DAYS

On account of many days cycling without stopping for such a break, we called 'time out' for 24 hours. Relief was the first sensation, partly due to the weather but mainly due to the call of "Thank You" from our thighs. The overnight change of weather, bringing in high winds, which would have played havoc with any cycling so the bus round the island was a real treat.

Eiders, red grouse, ravens and two whisky distilleries filled our day, plus planning. A storm was due on the coming Monday, when we were expecting to be camping on Colonsay. Giving up a prime desire was tough but essential. Colonsay would have to keep for another year.

The quirky two days on our first-ever trip to Islay could be remembered with fondness. We had resided beside the busy sea, just a few miles from the famed

101

Corryvreckan whirlpool that moved like no other I had seen before. That includes the Pentland Firth at The Orkneys and the meeting of The Tasman Sea and The Pacific at Wellington, but this was different. We watched it spin the three-masted "Flying Dutchman" like a matchbox on a fast stream. Even the Jura-Islay ferry needed to play seamanship games with the currents on every one of its regular crossings.

Untroubled Waters.
Malts with the help of a man called Pete

The Island's well being could be felt everywhere; there was no fear of crime, doors were never locked and people were pleasant. This, however, did not stop one of the poorly kept local cars smashing into the hotel's low garden wall after its handbrake failed while parked on a hill. It careered further down towards the quay only to be saved from the sea-dip by hitting and coming to rest on two other parked vehicles.

GIVEN A GOOD RECEPTION
The reason why The Port Askaig Hotel was the most expensive of our trip was location. It was not its modernity. The scenery and setting were splendid but the 1950s wallpaper gave it away. Last night, a guest on the first floor got up for a 3am wee only to put his foot through the ceiling and into the reception area below. Plans to wire it up with a light fitting or decorate the foot into the surroundings were not mentioned. We just saw the collapsed plaster and hole as we went for breakfast.

Yes, Islay captured one ankle as well as our hearts.

Saturday May 13th From Islay: Transition Day

Our plan had always been to cycle through The Outer Hebrides. To get there from Islay, necessitated a ferry back to the mainland and back out again. As I wrote earlier, Colonsay (of the Inner Hebrides) was to be omitted as a stop over, so we never got off the ferry when it called into that island but we met a snippet of its character by sailing close to half its eastern flank. Along with the other islands scattered on our way to Oban, the veil of sea mist, as low as 200ft, made them look more mysterious than ever.

Oban was merely a stop over, as it is for most who visit this hub for ferries. It deserves better than that but the draw of the islands is too great. Nestled in a giant horseshoe-shaped Firth of Lorn with the protection of Mull and Kerrera, it can hide from the ravages of raging seas, fooling travellers that any sea faring would be pleasurable. We had been gullible here on several occasions in the past.

We stopped for the Saturday night in order to take the Sunday ferry and to experience just how wonderful the oyster market can be in Oban.

Sun May 14th From Oban by ferry

An incoming depression out in the Atlantic made the crossing a bumpy one. We had never seen anyone sick on these ferries until this one. Nor had we seen such a pod of common dolphins in UK waters. The pod of around 25 rode with us in open sea for more than 10 minutes, clearly excited to be alongside our vessel. Judging by the many seabirds flying close by, they had been feeding before the ferry frolics took over. Earlier, we had seen shearwaters, petrels and a raft of razorbills, probably stocking up with food in the knowledge of the impending storm. We all know the natural world has a better sense of the weather than any meteorologist.

The romance of sailing into the islands, even on a huge CalMac ferry, was as wonderful as ever despite some green faces over the 5 hours. Castlebay on the southern end of the Outer Hebridean island of Barra may have been familiar to us but it was still enthralling. Anyone wondering why Barra's port is called Castlebay should see the castle in the bay. Built in 1039, Kisimul Castle was the fortress of The MacNeil clan and still is. We reacquainted ourselves with the town and its Co-Op (for possible storm provisions) before disappearing over the ridge on our short cycle to Brevig village in the late light of early summer.

Brevig was a bay rather than a true village on Barra's east coast. It contained a dozen properties, all visible in one scope and none more than 50 yards from another under a semi-circle of low fells. Meallard, our B&B was the furthest south and east, so it was the most protected from the storm that was to pen us in for two days.

That was: Oban-Barra in The Outer Hebrides by ferry-Castlebay-Brevig   3 miles

---

NICKNAMES

Cathy has never been labelled with a definitive pet name at home but I began reacting to the regions with local forms with accents to match"

Kent: Darling

London: Sweetie

Norf London: Darlin'

Cambridge: I did not dare because they were so Politically Correct that no reference to gender was allowed.

Fenland: with an East Anglian twang: Gal

Lincolnshire; Duck (Dourk)

Humberside: Luv

Yorkshire: Lass

Sunderland: Pet

Scottish Uplands: Lassie

Outer Hebrides: Lassie Doone

Monday 15th May Going nowhere

Happy Birthday, Dad R.I.P.

No ferries ran to Eriksay due to Force 11 winds. We managed a short evening stroll to see a seal, sheltering eiders, terns and a great northern diver (with the lovely Gaelic name of polochar).

Mairi, our host, let us have the run of the house while she worked and the bairns were at school, then squeezed us into her son's bedroom for the second night, so that others could be accommodated.

Mairi told us of her concern that "Stornaway Gaelic" (pronounced 'Garlic') was washing over her own dialect, native to Barra. She blamed the teachers 'imported' from Glasgow. It seamed ironic that the spread of the Gaelic language may lead to the loss of the richness within its diversity. We had heard Gaelic onwards from the Southern Uplands. It was never spoken intrusively (as if to avoid English ears) and, especially in song, was always sweet to the ear.

Tuesday 16th May From Brevig on Barra

With no certainty that the ferry would run, we, with 35 other cyclists descended from all parts, took the lashing rain and swirling wind on our panniers to wait in hope at Ardmore terminal. At points where the wind was broadside, we could only walk for fear of falling.

We were heading north. The theory on cycling The Outer Hebrides was to start at the southern island of Barra, then hop by ferry or causeway between the others. We had done this by car a few years ago and revisited twice

106

more, so we knew how it functioned, just never expected what we found on a bike!

The rocky 8-mile crossing on a small ferry, packed to the gunnels came as an obscure relief. In conversations with fellow cyclists showed their anticipation, trepidation and lunacy about "cycling The Outer Hebrides". We had these from Dover, of course, but we tried not to mention it. The first hill on Eriksay covered most of these emotions with only the submariner group cycling all the way up on account of having no luggage and young legs. The rest of us walked and pushed most of it.

Harsh winds shoved us around, so Am Politician, the real-life 'Whisky Galore' pub took our custom as the rain swept in. Of course, the submariners had preceded us, so the banter continued while the heavens opened to throw a turquoise blanket onto the inner shore-waters. These chaps spend 3 months underwater at a time on board Resolution class submarines with a Polaris missile for company. They told us they have two families: the wife and kids back home and (with a sweep of the arm) these guys. The cycle was one of their team-building fitness programmes.

From here, it was broken sun all the way but wind battered us brutally. Cathy walked the mile-long causeway between Eriksay and the next island, South Uist where the crosswind was capable of a sideway push either over the parapet or into the oncoming traffic. I walked with Cathy or cycled behind her because I was more confident in the wind, but I still sensed the danger. South Uist's early roads were westward and windward so, despite the flatness it too was difficult. Another unexpected inconvenience was the level of traffic on the narrow lanes. The system of passing places was all very well but the distance between them is set for car use, not slow touring bikes. We guessed May would be one of the busiest months on The Hebrides, and so it proved. We were invariably stopping on the narrow straits rather than making the car wait five minutes for us to cover a quarter of a mile in the wind. This meant that we often stopped on narrow verges between the passing places, either with a stone wall within inches or a steep drop and occasionally both. Once off the bike, there were times we could not get back on them due to hills/wind/another car/a chance to moan, therefore enforcing a walk. No bunnies were entirely joyous, but we were cheering each other on, with a healthy contribution from the land and seascapes.

Cheers rang out when we turned north and harnessed the wind. This turn took us away from our favoured haunt of The Polochar (you know what that means) Inn who were full of package-deal cyclists.

South Boisdale, our B&B location was a disparate community, as many Hebridean settlements are. A next-door neighbour could be two miles away, so a chat over the garden fence would involve a long walk first. The glory of our B&B, Ard Na Anach (High House) was its proximity to the machair, the grassy downs that grace the western sand dunes of these islands; loved by wild flowers and us.

That was:
Brevig on Barra-ferry to Eriksay-through Eriksay-South Uist- South Boisdale 15 miles

DECISION TIME

Yesterday's enforced rest day and this late afternoon had given us time to gather a great deal of information on any forward positions and options. Those options and considerations were as follows:

1) Finish at The Ness, on Lewis and sail from Stornaway. The weather forecasts dictated the need to hole-up in a B&B for a couple of days plus, once we got back to the mainland, there were no railway stations near Ullapool. Ullapool's only man-with-a-van who transfers cyclists to the nearest station was fully booked for the next two weeks.

2) Finish at Cape Wrath: The same weather problems plus the lone, pivotal hotels on the final 90 mile stretch (or 180 miles if you go both ways) were pre-booked in every room for weeks. No camping was allowed on the relevant estates and, anyway, they could not cater for any non-resident of the hotel. The same man-in-a-van issues stopped us, too.

3) ...the most romantic one.. Get the early morning ferry to Mallaig and take the most romantic train journey home.

We chose romance.

We felt wonderful once the mixed emotions of finality faded and we focused on our achievement. We had cycled from Dover to The Outer Hebrides! Wow!

Celebrations took place at The Borrowdale Arms Hotel, an exhilarating cycle ride away in evening sun exclusive to northern people. Local langoustines and tennis-ball sized scallops were washed down with Scotland's finest malty stuff. Fellow travellers swelled the takings and talked of daring do. I might have even wrangled a free fishing session on the Avimore Estate via one backpacker-ranger.

The famed late-night sun served us well on the lanes back to our B&B. Small lochs of an acre or two littered the flat lands. Their waters offered a deep-blue velvet colour in contrast to last year's bleached undergrowth and this year's grazing pastures. In a victorious mood and with cuckoos still calling in the wild, I let out a primeval yell to claim the world as my own. My love and admiration for Cathy had never been greater. This had been magical and was ending magically, if not as expected. Highly appropriately, we road two abreast, laughing and loving into the sunset.

The End of The Cycling....
But there is more...

The Team of Two

HOMEWARD

Wed May 17th
An alarm bell rang at 4.45am. At that time I was scoring
goals for England (again). Sadly, of those two sentences,
only one was fact. The 7am ferry from Loch Boisdale was
6 or 7 miles away and we were meant to be on it. Grey
skies and 40mph winds reinforced our decision to take
the opportunity for a beautiful departure.

Mallaig's hills embraced its port and our gay B&B hosts
were equally as welcoming. We walked the northern
ridge before a celebratory lunch (can't stop, can we?). It
was more Scottish seafood but with Italian pasta this
time. This formed the basis for an afternoon nap, aided
and abetted by Dr P. Grigio.

In the evening, the final surprise of the day was a large
tope, a cousin of the sharks, cutting the surface with its
recognisable dorsal fin just 3 yards from the rocks on the
shore

Thur May 18th
So, to the Mallaig train journey that swept us easily
through mountainous lands of untouched richness, then
alongside much of The West Highland Way that had
thrilled us in 2011. It was as if the weather wanted to
give us its best side by casting sun spotlights on its
grandest features. Ben Nevis wore an ermine stole and
lochs danced with sunshine diamonds. We knew how
rough these places could cut up, but from the safe
distance of a cuddle in a railway carriage, it was a
majestic picture.

A Scottish Farewell

In London

We arrived at Euston at 10pm, where there is no
"Disabled Lift" down to the tube train and walked to
King's Cross where they said there was. We are not
disabled (often) but the lifts were needed for our bikes,
which are not easy to get down escalators. There were
no streets paved with gold that night, just dark ones full
of slashing rain. Londoners flashed by with jackets over
heads while Cathy tried to weave this blind man through
the sort of conditions where I am prone to collisions.
Hazards akimbo. So fraught was my wife that, when
confronted with a station assistant who told here there
were no lifts, she yelled at him. I was aware of our need

to get down to the tube fast or we would miss the last train out of Liverpool Street, Cathy was in Red Mist-ville. "Stop shouting at me, " said the man. "Why are there no lifts? It says 'LIFTS'" yelled Cathy. "I will call the police for harassment," warned the man as things got heated. "Stop yelling at the man," I implore. She kept on. "Stop yelling at the man." He threatened her again. "Stop yelling at the man"....

We walked our bikes down the stairs and made the train. Two weeks later, Cathy calmed down.

The Route

The place-names indicate where we ended each day's cycle

The Outer Hebrides

South Boisdale

Brevig, Barra

Oban

Port Askaig, Islay

Lochranza — Ardrossan

Brodick — Maybole

Newton Stewart

Gatehose of Flee·

Castle Douglas — Annan

Wetheral — Haltwhistle

Long Newton

South Otterington

Linton —on-the-Ouse

Hexham

Newcastle

Sunderland

Riccal

Saltmarshe

Barnetsby

Barnsey

Boston

Wisbech

Little Downham

Cambridge

Clavering

Harlow

Greenwhich, London — Gravesend

Sittingbourne Faversham

Canterbury

Seasalter

Shepherdswell

Dover

114

Dover to Outer Hebrides Itinerary

Date	From	to	Miles en route
	Home	Dover	
24-Mar	Dover	Shepherdswell	6.5
25-Mar	Shepherdswell	Canterbury	11
26-Mar	Canterbury	Seasalter	11
27-Mar	Seasalter	Faversham	7.1
28-Mar	Faversham	Sittingbourne	22
29-Mar	Sittingbourne	Gravesend	22
30-Mar	Gravesend	Greenwich	32
31-Mar	Greenwich	Harlow	37
01-Apr	Harlow	Clavering	25
02-Apr	Clavering	Cambridge	25
06-Apr	Brain	Surgery	
19-Apr	Cambridge	Little Downham	29
20-Apr	Little Downham	Wisbech	25
21-Apr	Wisbech	Boston	36
22-Apr	Boston	Bardney	35
23-Apr	Bardney	Barnetsby	35
24-Apr	Barnetsby	Saltmarshe	35
25-Apr	Saltmarshe	Riccal	17
26-Apr	Riccal	Linton on the Ouse	24
27-Apr	Linton on the Ouse	South Otterington	32
28-Apr	South Oteerington	Long Newton	30
29-Apr	Long Newton	Sunderland	39

30-Apr	Sunderland	Newcastle	25
01-May	Newcastle	Hexham	25
02-May	Hexham	Haltwhistle	20
03-May	Haltwhistle	Wetheral	23
04-May	Wetheral	Annan	28
05-May	Annan	Castle Douglas	40
06-May	Castle Douglas	Gatehouse of Fleet	19
07-May	Gatehouse of Fleet	Newton Stewart	24
08-May	Newton Stewart	Maybole	38
09-May	Maybole	Brodick, Arran	40
10-May	Brodick, Arran	Lochranza	15
11-May	Lochranza	Port Askaig	7
12-May	Port Askaig	Oban	1
13-May	Oban	Barra, Outer Hebrides	4
14-May	Barra	South Uist	15
15-May	South Uist	Mallaig	6
16-May	Mallaig	Home	
	Totals		865.6

The extra miles cycled, mainly to and from stations, meant we topped the 900 miles in all.

Lessons Learnt

1. You always take too many clothes.
2. Expect injuries and bike failures.

3. The cycling community and cycle shops are brilliant.
4. Love your partner.
5. Expect it to get tough
6. Check to see who else is doing your trip or parts of it.
7. Be happy with your decisions
8. Question local knowledge
9. Question it again

KIT

What did we use?

Cheap gear ends up expensive, so we reconcile ourselves by spending good money on classy kit.

Paramo waterproofs (jackets and trousers); Vaude lightweight tent; two thermarest mattresses; 2 sleeping bags; comfortable trainers because we knew we would walk alot (Cathy); Flat, Long Distance trainers called Altra Zero Drop (me): Bridgedale Trekker and Darn Tough socks; 4 Vade panniers; a bum-bag for essentials; a layered approach of lightweight clothing (any brand). Tracksters and cycling shorts (ladies must not wear knickers, Cathy now knows) Petzl head torches.! A Sumsung Tough phone (not made anymore), Fountain Pen!!, Paper, Cards and Crib Board. No GPS, but an EE Wi-Fi hub that did not work in remote areas, an iPod but no pyjamas. Oh, and no worries.

The Aftertaste

Something as wonderful as a long journey takes a good while to sink in, so these notes cover the afterglow some 4 months on.

When we set off from Dover, we were hoping that Cathy would jog it and I would cycle in support. This morphed into the two-bike cycle thing. We had every intention of getting to Cape Wrath and there was some immediate disappointment when realism kicked in. Looking back, we are even more certain of our decision making. It helped too, that there was so much delight in closing the adventure at The Outer Hebrides. We will always look back at this as one of the best things we have ever done.

The Nation itself proved to be the winner: its people and its geography in fair proportion. Experiencing the magnitude of our landscape is very humbling and we sensed how insignificant we are and what a brief candle we burn. This world is massive and our Nation is but a minor part. What does that make me?

And I need to give the greatest accolade to my wife, Cathy. Quite apart from being the only living creature, beyond nits that would ever cohabit with me, she stands as a remarkable human being. She is:
- A lexicon of geographical terms
- An instinctive traveller
- Intimate with cartography and its contours
- My carer, my eyes and my love.

It was a beautiful thing to do together.

Thank you so much for joining us on our wonderful journey.

Cathy and Jim

Also by the author also published on Amazon:
Land's End to John O'Groats
The Thamespath Walk

cathyjim@btinternet.com

Printed in Great Britain
by Amazon